Shela's *Frequent Foreplay* relationship is on the rig... ....ay. whether flying solo or with a partner, let this book be your guide to a healthy relationship filled with satisfying intimacy and amazing emotional highs you'll be happy to brag about to your close friends.

Larry James,
Author of *How to Really Love the One You're With*

Shela Dean's fun and wise book provides a simple yet effective approach to giving the best of yourself to your partner every day. It's jam-packed with wonderful tips for bringing greater generosity, happiness and closeness to your relationship. Even the happiest couples will find nuggets of wisdom that will enrich their relationship.

Marci Shimoff,
NY Times bestselling author of *Happy for No Reason* and
Chicken Soup for the Woman's Soul

Informative and fun, insightful and practical, applicable to all couples—what else could you ask for in a relationship book?! *Frequent Foreplay Miles, Your Ticket to Total Intimacy* is a must read for anyone who wants a more joyously intimate relationship.

Mary Jo Rapini, L.C.P.
Co-author of *Start Talking & Is God Pink*,
Host of *Mind, Body & Soul with Mary Jo*
(Fox Morning News, Houston)

Shela spoke to the Executive Girlfriends' Group about her book. It was the most practical and everyday useful advice about relationships that I have ever heard.

Chicke Fitzgerald,
Founder, Executive Girlfriends' Group

I LOVE this concept! What a fantastic, easy-to-understand and FUN way to deal with some of the more serious issues all couples face.

Jennifer Whitlock,
Owner, The Help Desk Company

As a clinical psychologist for over 20 years, I often see individuals and couples who approach discussions about their relationship with a sense of dread, worried they will make matters worse by trying to let their partner know how they feel. As a result, they let small stresses and resentments build up until these pose a real threat to the relationship. Frequent Foreplay Miles provides a structure for couples to communicate with each other and understand one another's needs and preferences and, just as important, a sense of levity and lightness that allows them to enjoy the conversations and not take themselves quite so seriously.

Ann V. Deaton, PhD, PCC,
DaVinci Resources

This is definitely a book that I, as a marital therapist, would recommend to couples who are looking for a way to be closer and more in touch with each other so they can be the responsive partners they want to be, communicate with greater clarity, and together create a joyful and solid relationship that can withstand the challenges all couples face.

Wendy Kopald, LCSW

Shela's ideas are a great way to re-ignite a relationship and get couples communicating. If you've ever been in a relationship, you'll get right away what she's talking about. You'll also appreciate the opportunity to think again about what really matters to you and to learn what matters most to the person you love. I know I did, and I've been married over 30 years.

Plum Cluverius, PCC
Executive Coach, Vedere Consulting

frequent foreplay miles®

Your Ticket to Total Intimacy

Shela Dean

the Peppertree Press

Sarasota, Florida

For information regarding permission,
call 941-922-2662 or contact us at our website:
www.peppertreepublishing.com or write to:
the Peppertree Press, LLC.
Attention: Publisher
1269 First Street, Suite 7
Sarasota, Florida 34236

ISBN: 978-1-936051-28-1

Library of Congress Number: 2009935776

Printed in the U.S.A.

Printed September 2009

This book is dedicated to my husband Dale Dean, who—after all these years—still takes my breath away.

Table of Contents

Acknowledgments

Writing a book is a daunting task. It is both a solitary endeavor and a team effort. I am brought to my knees in gratitude at the thought of all the people who supported me, who believed in me, and whose encouragement kept me going.

To the many friends who cheered me on, a giant, heartfelt thank you. The list is long. So forgive me if I leave it at, "You know who you are." And, yes, you may all come to Oprah with me. Now, will somebody please tell Oprah to book me?

Thanks to my ex-husband Carl (last name withheld to protect his privacy) for his willingness to share our story. Carl, you've always been one of the good guys.

A special thanks and a giant hug to Ferrell Anne Jennings who, since the early days of our writers' group, has believed in and loved me. Anne, the value of your friendship cannot be measured. If everyone had a friend as generous, supportive, and loyal as you, the world would be a better place.

This book wouldn't exist without the professional guidance and loving friendship of Libby Gill who has my undying gratitude for both. Libby, I am honored to call you my friend. Even more so, that you call me yours.

My sister Jenny Romanelli is the best sister ever. She's also a wonderful friend. Jenny, thanks for always understanding. My brother David Woosley has been my most ardent cheerleader. Dave, you're the greatest. To Jenny, Dave and to other family members, especially Brian Woosley and his children, Bill Fisher, Bill Romanelli, Ann Woosley, Michelle Woosley, Jennifer Lynn, Bill Banghart, and Hazel Banghart, my thanks and my love.

Life is a never-ending joy because of my too-adorable-to-be-believed granddaughters Addison Julia Fisher and Kennedy Nicole Fisher, the cutest kids on the planet. Baby A and Special K, you are the light of my life. I adore you.

I am blessed to have Lisa Cook as my daughter. She is the best kid a mom can have, and the best friend a girl can have. Lisa, I am button-bursting proud of you and the woman you have grown up to be. You and the girls sacrificed Mom and Mimi time so I could write. Thank you. I love you times a trillion to the tenth power plus a bag of jellybeans!

I struck gold the day I met my husband Dale Dean. Dale, you taught me to see life through generous eyes. Without that gift, this book wouldn't exist and my life would be far less rich. For all the meals you brought to my desk so I could keep working, for all the days you spent alone while I wrote, for the movies you watched by yourself, for the unflagging encouragement, for your undying and unquestioned support, for your ear, heart and shoulder, for your willingness to let me tell our story, for doing the laundry so I'd always have clean underwear, for taking the cat to the vet, taking my car to the gas station for fill-ups, picking up my prescriptions, and all the thousands of ways—big and small—that you cleared the way for me to write this book I am eternally grateful. I am crazy mad in love with you.

And, finally, a huge thanks to those professionals who, because of their brilliant editing, suggestions, and marketing, design, photographic and publishing savvy made this book better: Carole Greene and Jacqueline Simenauer of the Simenauer-Greene Literary Agency; Vicki St. George of Just Write Now; Julie Ann Howell of Peppertree Press; Jodi Deros of ATOMDesign; Dominique Attaway of Dominique Attaway Photography; and editor S. R. Maxeiner, Jr.

Foreword

by Libby Gill

As a corporate entertainment executive at Sony, Universal and Turner Broadcasting, I spent fifteen years in senior leadership roles managing relationships with stakeholders, celebrities and CEOs. Though managing professional relationships could be challenging, they were a breeze compared to my personal ones. If only Shela had been in my life during my marriage, divorce, and subsequent re-entry into single life, things would have been a lot easier. Fortunately, I've got her in my life now. And through her terrific book, *Frequent Foreplay Miles*, you can have this wise and witty woman in your life, too.

Now, as an executive coach and branding strategist, I guide individuals and organizations to articulate their authentic value to a crowded marketplace. I had the good fortune to lead the original PR team that helped establish the Dr. Phil brand, which celebrated the most successful launch of a daytime show since the debut of Oprah. During my tenure with Dr. Phil, I not only heard the relationship issues that people brought to the show on a regular basis, but the advice that Dr. Phil gave his guests and the recommendations offered by a range of relationship experts. And, as a coach myself, I regularly rub elbows with some amazing relationship coaches. Shela Dean is definitely in that league.

In my book *You Unstuck: Mastering the New Rules of Risk-Taking in Work and Life*, I look at people who have let their fears keep them stuck in negative behavior patterns, including unsatisfying relationships. Climbing out of a relationship rut is no easy task if you are weighed down by grudges and resentment. As Shela so aptly explains, most of the grudges and resentment we harbor are based on misperception, misunderstanding, and a lack of knowledge about what makes our partner tick—and sometimes about what makes us tick. Shela shows you how to unravel misperceptions, heal the damage, avoid misunderstandings in the days ahead, and best of all, build on your God-given differences to strengthen your relationship into one that can withstand the test of time.

The Foreplay Back-Pocket Guide, consisting of four deceptively simple questions, is one of the most effective tools that I have been pleased to add to my coaching repertoire. Not only is it invaluable in guiding you to the right course of action in your primary relationship, it's incredibly useful in helping you navigate any relationship, from friends to family to co-workers.

Whether you want to move a shaky relationship to solid ground, rekindle a flickering flame of attraction or take a good relationship to great, you'll get the help you need. As an added bonus, this book is a heck of a lot of fun for both men (yes, men!) and women.

Shela has an uncanny ability to make complex concepts easy to understand and even easier to apply to everyday life. Her practical meat-and-potatoes approach, combined with humor and insight, and capped off with a "cut to the chase" energy, makes it fun to embark on her do-it-yourself relationship improvement course.

Poets, scientists and scholars may have written a billion words about love, but *Frequent Foreplay Miles* brings a fresh perspective to the topic of intimate relationship bliss that you can put into play today. I know you'll find this book as insightful and entertaining as I did. Use it frequently!

Introduction

When I was a kid, moron jokes were the rage—the words "politically" and "correct" had not yet been joined at the hip. I laughed until, in the jargon of the time, I nearly busted a gut over such silliness as, "Why did the moron tiptoe past the medicine cabinet?" Answer: "He didn't want to waken the sleeping pills."

By seventh grade I was far too sophisticated for moron jokes. I had discovered Nancy Drew. I read and re-read every book in the series and, oh how I wanted to be just like Nancy, a girl detective with Ned Nickerson as my boyfriend. By high school my nose was buried in *Gone with the Wind* and my go-to-sleep fantasies involved Rhett Butler who, to this day, makes me swoon.

Fast forward to May 28, 1994. I was packing my things, moving out of the home I had shared with my husband

and thinking how relieved I was that the relationship was over. I taped the box shut and, out of the blue, this popped into my head: "Why did the moron keep hitting himself in the head with a hammer?" Answer: "Because it felt so good when he stopped."

An Aha! Moment—an epiphany inspired by a cardboard box and a long-forgotten moron joke. I had a string of failed relationships, culminating with this failed marriage. I had gotten it wrong so many times that on that day in 1994 I had the scary and sobering thought that perhaps I went into relationships just to feel good about getting out of them. One thing was for sure: It was time to stop hitting myself in the head with a hammer. It was time to stop being a moron. Next time, I promised, I would get it right. And I did—but more about that later.

Implied in "getting it right the next time" is that there is a next time. The sheets were barely cool from my failed marriage and, here I was, thinking about the next one. I wanted to do it again. I wanted to be part of a couple. We all do. We're built that way.

Larry King has seven marriages to six women—yep, he married one of them twice. Mickey Rooney and Liz Taylor are tied at 8 marriages each. If these three don't prove that no matter how many times we mess up, we're hardwired to pair up, I don't know what does. Okay. Arguably, they are proof that some people never learn. Valid point. But consider this: Barbara DeAngelis, recognized expert on marriage and relationships, has been married at least four times, once to John Gray, author of *Men Are From Mars, Women Are From*

Venus. John has been married twice and a hearty congratulations to him and his wife Bonnie who just celebrated their 25th wedding anniversary. I've failed at marriage, too. Even we "experts" get it wrong before we get it right.

So compelling is the human urge to mate, we do it over and again until we drop dead, are too exhausted to lift our heads, settle for what we have—even when what we have is unfulfilling or painful—or Hallelujah! get it right. Given the strength of the coupling urge, you'd think Mother Nature would have been more generous in doling out relationship survival skills. Forget it. You're on our own. And just when you think you've got it knocked, you're blindsided by a curve ball. Well, that's why there are books like this, written by people who, like me, have figured it out (at least for themselves) and who hope what they've learned will help you do the same.

I don't promise or even pretend to have all the answers for everybody. All I can do is tell you my story, give you my thoughts, and share a strategy I think will work for you because it worked for my sweetheart and me. But people—and the relationships they enter—are unique in a hundred zillion ways. What you take from this book will be different from that of every other reader, but you and all other readers have one thing in common: you want a Totally Intimate relationship—in and out of the bedroom. I'll do my best to guide you, but it's up to you to do the heavy lifting. Expecting results by reading this or any other book without doing the work is like standing at the gym door, staring at the equipment, and expecting to get in shape. It's not going to happen. I know. I've tried. And, by the way, the work you need to do is on *yourself*, not on your partner. If you want this book to help you "fix" your sweetheart, put it down right now. It's up to your sweetie to do his or her own heavy lifting and to decide what needs fixing and then do it. You need to do the same.

Now, a word about my background:

I didn't start out to be a relationship coach. I didn't get a degree in psychology. The letters MSW, LCSW, or PhD aren't strung after my name. The letters that follow my name are JD, which stands for Juris Doctor. That's right. I'm a lawyer. To 99.9% of the population, "Attorney as Relationship Coach" is an oxymoron! I get it. But hold on . . .

During my entire 20-year career, I never once chased an ambulance to the ER, bribed a city official, used a loophole to get a miscreant out of jail, or said, "Sue the bastard!" Every moron joke I ever heard or told as a kid, and plenty more, has been retold by substituting the word "lawyer" for "moron." We're called many names, most of them unflattering. The name I prefer is "Counselor at Law," with emphasis on "counselor."

I wanted to serve my clients in a positive way so I chose estate planning as my practice area. You might think that writing wills and trusts is cut and dried, just a bequeath here and a bequeath there. You'd be wrong. Every estate plan is as unique as the person or couple for whom it's done. Just as life is dynamic, so is an estate plan. It requires updating and modification as circumstances change. I had long-term, close working relationships with many of my clients. I worked with couples of all ages and at all stages of life. I found myself faced with a myriad of issues having to do not just with legal matters but also with how couples relate to each other. Like doctors, attorneys are often the only ones outside a relationship to know when things are bad and getting ready to crack. I saw the impact of both big and small issues on relationships: everything from birth and death, addiction, infidelity and illness, to who put the dent in the car or burned the toast that morning.

I was called on to counsel my clients at critical and often stressful points in their lives—marriage, divorce, a loved one's death, loss of health or wealth, the blending of families. I felt I needed to understand the dynamics of relationships. I studied everything I could get my hands on to become an expert. Before long, I was counseling my clients on personal matters as well as on legal matters.

The majority of relationship books I read were thick with theory and psychobabble, based on gender stereotypes, meant for seriously broken relationships, or so generic as to be inapplicable to most couples. I wanted a book that was non-therapeutic, practical and fun, applicable to everyday life and the issues all couples face. Little did I know that my life's path would lead me to write that very book.

We use lots of good words to describe the one we love. I've pretty much stuck to "sweetheart" and "partner" and if I've overused them, my apologies. This book is for anyone in a relationship, however you may define that, and all synonyms refer to the object of your affection regardless of the term you use to describe your significant other.

I want for you what I have: a fulfilling, Totally Intimate relationship and the joy that comes with it. My husband Dale and I don't get it right all the time. We're not perfect and you won't be either. Good news. You don't have to be.

With love,

Shela

1
Foreplay:

It's Not Just About Sex

**In the end, the love you take
is equal to the love you make.**
—Paul McCartney & John Lennon

It began twelve years ago over morning coffee and cinnamon toast. Dale, my husband, was always late. It always annoyed me. I had gently suggested, then nagged, to no avail. On that day I had an inspiration. I would put it in a context he would understand: SEX! I smiled sweetly, pointed my butter knife at him for emphasis, and said, "Dale, you need to know something about being in a relationship:

foreplay is all day, every day, 24/7. It includes anything and everything that affects how I feel about you. So here's an idea for you. Try racking up Frequent Foreplay Miles by being on time. The more miles you rack up, the more 'in the mood' I'll be."

We laughed, but Dale got it and, in his sexual self-interest, pledged to become the on-time guy. After breakfast he earned Frequent Foreplay Miles by wiping the table free of toast crumbs. I earned mine by ironing his shirt. Our good-bye kiss was especially sweet. The sheets sizzled that night, and in the afterglow we acknowledged that the simple idea expressed in our morning's playful exchange had legs. It became our philosophy to earn as many and lose as few Frequent Foreplay Miles as possible. We had fun with it. When I made Dale a tuna fish sandwich or he emptied the trash, we made sure we got our Frequent Foreplay Miles. Before long it was an integral part of our life. Laughter was the hallmark of our relationship. We were the couple others envied. We were so easily happy and fit so naturally together, we thought it would never change.

We were wrong.

Because of a business partnership that went bad, we suffered a financial setback that turned our idyllic life on its head. Faced with the loss of our financial security, we left the life we loved in California and moved to Richmond, Virginia. Dale and I are adventurous people. We arrived in Virginia with our sense of adventure intact. I would build a business and Dale, as part of our economic recovery, would remodel our "new" 80-year-old, long-neglected Tudor that was the evil twin to our beautiful California home. We said it would be fun. And it was—for a little while.

Our furniture would not arrive for several weeks. We moved into the house with our cat Sophie still drugged from the Benadryl that kept her calm on the plane from California, a coffee pot, towels and bed linens, work clothes, and a blowup bed. I had the foresight to pack a repair kit for the bed, but we were never able to find the pinhole leak that caused it to slowly deflate. Every night, about 2 a.m., we would wake nose-to-nose in the sagging middle, wrestle with that giant-balloon-of-a-bed to pull ourselves to the edge, blow it back up, then spend a few minutes giggling— or a lot of minutes doing something else—before going back to sleep.

Our days were spent working on the house. While Dale gutted the kitchen, I stripped paint. We made jokes about the pinhole leak and its effect on our middle-of-the-night sex life. When wasps as big and as mean as fighter jets invaded our house, we took turns shooting them with bug spray and competing over body count. We bought a small TV at Costco and watched the 2004 election results as we sat on the floor eating grilled cheese sandwiches cooked on the electric skillet that was our kitchen. The Richmond International Raceway is a few miles from our house. On race night, we'd open all the windows and listen to the live roar of the engines as we watched on the muted TV. As lifelong residents of California, we were weather weenies. Thunder and lightning, common in Virginia, had us out on the porch holding hands, watching in awe.

There were good times. But we were alone in Richmond and missed lifelong friends. We were no longer able to travel or afford the things that had made our life enjoyable. The remodeling project quickly became overwhelming. Before long, we began to grieve for the life we had loved and lost. That grief spilled over into our relationship. One day, as we made our billionth trip to Home Depot, it hit me. We weren't talking. It was quiet in the car. We, who had so often vied for airtime, had run out of things to say. I searched for a way to jumpstart the conversation. Nothing. I was too sad, too depressed, too emotionally tired. Dale was too. The joy and laughter we once shared had given way to feelings of disappointment and individual guilt over the circumstances that had led to our move. Our sadness bordered on depression. We were no longer having fun. We were drifting apart.

I'll be honest. I wondered whether we would make it. As I look back, I am convinced that our marriage survived because long before our financial woes we had made a conscious decision to bank those Frequent Foreplay Miles. We continued to do the "little things" that kept our FFM accounts full. Dale still brought morning coffee to me. I still put his laundry away. He noticed when I finished a book and bought me another of the legal thrillers I am addicted to. I had his car washed. Those small acts of kindness were reminders of our "for better or worse" pledge to take care of each other, reminders that kept us focused on easing the other's pain. We weren't perfect. Like all relationships, ours is not free of wounds. And like most people who face adversity, we weren't always at our best. We made Frequent Foreplay Miles "withdrawals" by being testy, grumpy, irritable and, sometimes downright disagreeable, but because we started with a high balance and continued to add to that balance, our Frequent Foreplay Miles accounts were always in the black.

Most importantly, as a byproduct of our philosophy, we had established mutual trust. As we worked through the challenge we felt safe expressing our thoughts, our doubts, our fears, and our hopes, even when what one of us said was difficult for the other to hear. The joy and the laughter eventually came back. By staying true to our Frequent Foreplay Miles philosophy, we emerged as a stronger, more committed couple. The intimacy we now share—in and out of the bedroom—is richer and better than ever for having faced down the challenge.

Frequent Foreplay Miles. It started as a bit of a joke, nothing more than my playful way of making a point to Dale. It became a philosophy of marriage that sustained us through a major challenge. From there, it has evolved into what it is today—a strategy that will help you have Total Intimacy. That is when:

- You are so connected in mind and heart you feel a physical bond;

- It's totally cool to share your most private thoughts, needs and desires;

- You are 24/7 cheerleaders—nurturing, loving, and supportive—so you become the best that you can be;

- You trust that even when mess-ups happen, you've both acted with good intentions; and

- As an added bonus, you want to jump each other's bones at every opportunity!

The odds: they're not in your favor.

Total Intimacy. It's what every couple wants. Sadly, even two people who are seemingly made for each other have better than even odds of sitting in divorce court wondering what in the heck happened. Why? What *does* happen? To answer that question, let's start at the beginning.

Falling in love is a hormone-induced high you hope will never end. You count the minutes until you see him again. You call just to hear her sweet voice. The air is alive with the snap, crackle and pop of sexual energy. Your friends are bored silly with your ceaseless yammering about the Perfect 10 who, can you believe it, is mad about you, too. He lets you pick the Saturday night movie and you extrapolate that small generosity into a generalization about what a giving person he is, not at all like the self-centered jerk you used to date. You think it's adorable when she jumps into the middle of your story and finishes it for you. You exaggerate that little habit into proof she's the soul mate who understands you in a way your self-absorbed ex never did. When you're together, everything else fades into oblivion.

Love may be blind but it's not completely senseless. No sooner have the words "Mr. Perfect" left your lips when you realize he lets you pick Saturday night's film because that's his opportunity to catch up on sleep. Your buddies are still sniggering over your confession that being a bachelor isn't all that great when you realize she never misses the chance to turn the spotlight on herself.

Nature is sneaky. Cupid needs time to take aim. To give him that time, your vision goes temporarily wacko. You can't see anything about your new love except good stuff. But Nature is also pretty darned smart. If people forever had their heads in the clouds, no one would have the focus to find the cure for the common cold or end global warming, much less take care of daily business. It's a dirty trick. I agree. But once Cupid's arrow is firmly embedded, your vision goes back to normal. You realize that some of the qualities you found so adorable and so reassuring are habits (or full-on personality flaws) that drive you teeth-clenching crazy. You find yourself complaining about what hurts your feelings, drives you nuts, or disappoints you. Your love engines, which have been running at maximum capacity, cool down to a comfortable running speed so you can be in love and function at the same time. And let's be honest: it's a relief when your sweetheart's imperfections give you permission to be a little less perfect yourself. Being on best behavior is like holding in your stomach. You can't do it forever and it feels sooooooooooooo good when you finally let go!

Restored vision is your wake-up call.

Once your vision is restored, you see your partner's previously invisible flaws as though under a giant spot light. At the same time, you paradoxically assume that he or she remains blind as a newborn kitten. Here's a 411 for you: each time you've had the realization that your sweetheart isn't perfect, your sweetheart has had the same realization about you. You think you're perfect. Your mother thinks you're perfect. Your sweetie does not. What's more, if you knew all the ways in which you seem imperfect, you'd be shocked. Do you think he has deplorable taste in art, talks too loudly on a cell phone, and needs a new wardrobe? Then don't be surprised if he thinks you wear your hair too long, can't tell a joke, and have an annoying machine-gun laugh. Each time you inwardly roll your eyes or cringe at something your partner says or does, remember this humbling fact: *Your partner is doing the same thing.*

It's tempting to believe that unless you hear otherwise, everything is super peachy keen. However, you'd better take a dose of reality before your sweetheart brings your flaws to your oh-so-shocked notice, or you do the same to him or her. Ask yourself these questions:

- Do you sometimes get irritated with or are embarrassed by your sweetheart yet keep it to yourself?

- Has your sweetheart hurt your feelings, disappointed you, or made you angry, but you didn't say a word?
- Does your sweetie have a habit that makes you crazy and you've never once complained?

You answered yes to all those questions. I know you did. Come on, admit it. You want to scream when she clicks her teeth on the ice cream spoon. You were steamed when he returned your car littered with fast-food wrappers. It hurt your feelings that she forgot to introduce you to a co-worker or he forgot the anniversary of your first date. Your sweetheart is blissfully unaware of your private critical thoughts. Your sweetie is clueless about those occasions when you smile outwardly but are suffering inwardly. Given that, isn't it likely that your sweetheart has private thoughts about you and also suffers in silence? Of course it is.

If you were emotional, intellectual, and experiential twins, it would be a heck of a lot easier to keep each other smiling internally and externally. But you're not. Each of you came to the relationship with a unique and vastly complex set of preferences, opinions, priorities, standards, points of view, and sensitivities, shaped by your DNA, upbringing, education, life's experience, religious or philosophical training, culture, and self-perception. All of that combines to form what I call your personal operating system, or, in the context of this book your *Foreplay Navigator*™. We all have one. It is the guide for how we see things and how we navigate life and our primary relationship. It is how we determine if others are flying right, including (perhaps especially) our life partner.

The Foreplay Navigators of you and your sweetheart overlap in fundamental ways or you wouldn't be a couple in the first place. They also differ in a zillion ways. Need proof? Think about the many ways in which you and your sweetie butt heads, step on each other's toes, and cross wires. Here's what those terms mean.

Butt Heads: A relationship is a never-ending process of negotiating the big and the small moments in which someone "wins" and someone "loses." Making joint decisions often results in head butting because each of you has a perspective based solely upon your own Foreplay Navigator. You may agree on going out to dinner, but unless you go to the food court at the mall, if one wants Chinese and the other wants Mexican, someone wins and someone loses. You might agree on having a baby but disagree on whether it should be raised Jewish or Baptist. Getting a pet sounds like a good idea, but agreeing on Rex or Fluffy, long or short hair, may require divine intervention. The list of ways in which couples can disagree and the things couples must negotiate is endless. For instance:

- How should birthdays and special events be celebrated?
- How should laundry be separated, washed and folded?
- Should your kids go to private or public school?

- Should the silverware go in the drawer to the left or to the right of the dishwasher?
- Should you decorate with carpet or hardwood floors, contemporary or traditional furniture?
- Is it better to replace the transmission in your current car or buy a new one?
- Should the bedroom window be cracked or wide open at night?
- How big should the TV be and where should it be placed?
- What movie to go see?
- Should the baby be named Susie or Gwendolyn?
- Does the Super Bowl trump your mother-in-law's 90th birthday party?
- Do tickets to the opera trump poker night?
- Should vacations be restful or adventurous?
- Does the bed need to be made every morning or the sheets changed every week?
- Should the dog be allowed to sleep on the bed?
- Is adding GPS to the new car a wise use of money?

And so on and so on ad infinitum.

All of these situations and many more are opportunities for two perfectly sane people to become insanely set in their own ideas and to get a lot of migraines from butting heads!

Step on Toes: You are bound to mess up if you don't know that according to your sweetheart's Foreplay Navigator:

- Dog-earring the pages of a book is a mortal sin.

- It's an act of treason to jump on the punch line of your partner's joke.

- Having coffee with an ex who blew into town is tantamount to cheating.

- Using the pet name "Snookie" in front of friends is a violation of privacy.

- A gift certificate is the ultimate I-gave-this-no-thought acknowledgment of a special occasion.

Yet violations of such unexpressed rules have doomed more relationships than blatant infidelity. Most of us know that sleeping around won't be tolerated, but most of us don't know—until we learn the hard way—that for our partner not calling every night we're on the road without her, or scheduling anything during football season without several weeks' notice, or letting the cat lick the ice cream bowl, is almost as bad. Worse yet, the cumulative effect of many such instances can get us in serious trouble without our ever knowing what we've done to make our sweetie angry. It's like stepping on a toe that's already sore and swollen: the least little pressure results in a yell of pain.

Cross Wires: Most couples talk about and are able to resolve (or learn to live with) the big stuff. It's the little stuff, what I call the "Dumb Stuff," that is so insidiously dangerous to a relationship because that's the stuff to which we so often give a negative (but usually wrong) spin. For instance:

- You say, "The rice is salty," and she hears, "You're a terrible cook."

- You leave a half-empty Starbucks cup in the car and he thinks, "She doesn't appreciate how hard I work to provide nice things."

- You fail to notice a new hairdo and she concludes you're no longer paying attention.

- You paint the bathroom and he points out the one missed spot, "proving" he thinks you're incompetent.

Most partners suffer the Dumb Stuff in silence because they believe they should pick their battles, it's better to avoid the conflict, or to complain will seem petty. However, it is exactly this same stuff that leads to grudges and long-term resentment based on nothing more than differing Foreplay Navigators. Let me give you an example that occurred in my marriage.

I continued to work outside the home after Dale retired. Dale, a gregarious people guy, would be alone much of the day. Happy to see me, he would start chatting the moment I walked in. As I listened I would thumb through the mail. One day he stopped mid-sentence and said, "I'll wait for you to finish." Whoops! According to his Foreplay Navigator I was not flying right. He interpreted my behavior as a lack of interest in what he was saying. He felt ignored and unimportant. I was accustomed to multitasking at the office and to being around others who did the same. If Dale had thumbed through the mail while I talked, I wouldn't have thought a thing of it. I love my husband. He's the last person on the planet I want to hurt, yet I had unknowingly done so, apparently many times over. In giving me feedback that allowed me to change my behavior, Dale supported me in being a more responsive partner. Better yet, we found a win-win solution. He would give me a few minutes to decompress, check the mail, and change into more comfortable clothes. I would then give him my undivided attention.

The little stuff counts.

Thumbing through the mail while your partner is chatting may not be a crime, *but any behavior that evokes a negative emotion damages the relationship.* The cumulative effect can be lethal. Ask anyone if infidelity can destroy a relationship and the answer will be, "Of course!" as if you had asked the stupidest question in the history of mankind. Ask the same person if once forgetting your sweetheart's birthday can destroy a relationship and the answer is likely to be, "Of course not!" as if you had asked the second most stupid question in the history of mankind. That person would be wrong. It's true that not even the most demanding partner is likely to split over one forgotten birthday. It's also true that even the strongest love can suffer death by a thousand cuts.

A forgotten birthday may be the last in a long string of hurts and disappointments that, while not individually fatal, cumulatively sap the life out of a once vibrant relationship. Too many cuts and the relationship risks bleeding to death or becoming too weak to withstand the unexpected challenges all relationships face. Head butts, stepped on toes, and crossed wires—no matter how individually small and insignificant—cause wounds to the relationship and destroy intimacy.

As an estate-planning attorney and as a relationship expert, I've seen far too many relationships crumble because of unshared rules, unexpressed desires, and unresolved differences in Foreplay Navigators. Head butts, stepped on toes, and crossed wires play havoc with intimacy—in and out of the bedroom. Who hasn't gone to bed with some simmering grudge and turned a back to the sweetheart who is left wondering why? We too often engage in a lose-lose match with little chance of a long-term relationship, much less long-term happiness. Imagine how much stronger, happier, and more intimate your relationship would be if you had a better understanding of each other's Foreplay Navigator, and the tools to identify and heal the wounds that result when your Foreplay Navigators are out of sync. That's exactly why I've written this book. By using Frequent Foreplay Miles any couple can create Total Intimacy, build a stronger, more passionate relationship and enjoy their trip through the friendly and not-so friendly skies of life. It's fun. It's sexy. It's easy. And it works!

Whether you and your sweetie do this together or you're embarking on a "relationship improvement course" on your own, applying the Frequent Foreplay Miles strategy will make your relationship richer, deeper, more intimate, sexier, and a whole lot more fun.

You won't be a perfect sweetheart. No one is, even if we could marry ourselves! But by understanding and then tailoring your behavior to fulfill your sweetheart's Foreplay Navigator, *you will be a less imperfect sweetheart.* When you know what your partner wants and do your best to give it (and as an added bonus, have fun doing it) you create a relationship that will joyfully stand the test of time.

Take a moment to think about something your sweetheart did that made you think you're the luckiest person on the planet. Now (without worrying about how many... we'll get to that later) drop a bunch of Frequent Foreplay Miles into your sweetheart's account. Doesn't that feel good?

Exercise

To help you apply what you've learned, I'd like you to complete this exercise. All you need is paper and pen. In Part A, you'll list times when you and your partner have butted heads, your sweetheart has stepped on your toes, and you've drawn a negative inference from something your sweetie has said or done. Then, in Part B you'll make a list of ways in which your sweetheart has been kind or thoughtful.

Go back in time as far as you need to.

Keep your list. You'll be using it for other exercises.

Part A

Head Butts: List ten ways in which you and your partner have butted heads. Each incident may be a forehead tap or a serious horn-locking. It doesn't matter whether you reached agreement or not. For example, "My sweetheart and I butted heads over how much money to spend on my best friend's wedding gift."

Stepped on Toes: List five times when your sweetheart did or said something that, according to your Foreplay Navigator, is inappropriate or just downright wrong. For example, "My toes were stepped on when my sweetheart included an ex on an email joke distribution list." Again, it can but doesn't have to be big and significant.

Crossed Wires: List five occasions when you gave a negative inference to something your sweetheart said or did. For example, "I was hurt when my sweetheart repainted the front door after I had painted it. It made me feel like my sweetheart thought I hadn't done a good job."

Part B

List 10 or more ways in which your sweetheart was thoughtful, kind, generous, or otherwise did something that made you feel a positive emotion, whether that emotion was relief, pleasure, delight, or over-the-moon excitement. Consider those times when your sweetheart did "right" what you think he or she often does "wrong." Include the emotion you felt, and how you might or did reciprocate. For example, "When my sweetheart surprised me with a cherry pie, I was delighted. I suggested (or might have suggested) we get two forks, put a big slice on one plate, and eat it in bed."

*2
Frequent Foreplay Miles:
Your Path to a Beautiful Flight

> *Marriage is not just spiritual communion,*
> *it is also remembering to take out the trash.*
> —Joyce Brothers

Frequent Foreplay Miles is both a philosophy and a process.

The philosophy is this: *You get Frequent Foreplay Miles when you fly right; you lose them when you don't. The more you have, the happier your relationship will be, so rack 'em up at every opportunity and avoid losing them whenever possible.*

If you do nothing more than incorporate that philosophy into your relationship, you'll be better off. Your Foreplay Back-Pocket Guide™, discussed in the next chapter, will help you do just that.

However, it's through the process of tracking Frequent Foreplay Miles that the philosophy becomes second nature and the benefits are more fully realized. There are detailed instructions on how to track in Chapter 4. Before you get started, let's review ten reasons why it just makes darned good sense to integrate Frequent Foreplay Miles—the philosophy and the process—into your relationship.

Reason #1: You learn to see every occasion as an opportunity for foreplay.

Just as great foreplay is essential to Wow! sex, great emotional foreplay is essential to a Wow! relationship. If Katie is in the mood for a romp, will she show up in the black stilettos that rev Mike's engines or the comfy old slippers she's usually schlepping around in? Talk about a no-brainer. She'll slip into those stilettos and it won't matter if she can't walk in them. Walking isn't what's on her mind and it won't be what's on his!

Great emotional foreplay is much the same. Consistently doing those things that jibe with your partner's Foreplay Navigator and consciously trying to win Frequent Foreplay Miles results in the Wow! relationship you want. Every occasion is an opportunity to pick up a few FFM. Going to Costco? Toss a jar of his favorite licorice into the basket. Hear the garage door open? Uncork a bottle of her favorite wine and greet her with a glass. Is her college roommate coming for a visit? Pick up flowers for the guest room. Is his softball team in the championship play-off? Go to the game and shout your head off.

Foreplay is all day, every day, 24/7. It includes everything and anything that affects how you feel about each other. Want sex tonight? Start the foreplay this morning. Want greater intimacy in your whole relationship? Start the emotional foreplay now and never stop. Doing little things for each other is a great way to pick up Frequent Foreplay Miles but is, by no means, the only way. As you'll learn in the next chapter, even dicey situations that might otherwise turn into arguments are opportunities to earn Frequent Foreplay Miles.

Reason #2: You develop the habit of constructive candor.

In Chapter 1 you learned how easily and how often innocent clashes of Foreplay Navigators result in hurt feelings and misunderstandings. When this happens, the usual responses are:

- *Suffering in silence.* The problem with this approach is that unaired grievances run the risk of morphing into grudges and long-term resentment.

- *Suffering out loud.* The problem with this approach is that knee jerk responses, complaining, nagging, criticism, and pouting with heavy sighs, are heard as and are about as effective as "blah-blah-blah."

A far better approach is what I call constructive candor. Here's an example of why it's so important. I was chatting with Jack and Denise, participants in my newly-wed focus group, about one of her tracker entries. Here's how the conversation went:

Shela: Denise, I see you dinged Jack for something he said about a class he was teaching. Can you tell me about that?

Denise: Jack and I are teachers at the same school. He had an all-day archery class on Saturday. Lots of students had enrolled. The class was going to be a handful so I offered to help. He said, "No."

Shela: Were your feelings hurt that Jack didn't accept your offer?

Denise: Yes! I thought he didn't think I was good enough to help him teach the class. That not only hurt my feelings but, frankly, made me angry. I really resented it.

Shela: Jack, why did you say, "No," and did you know Denise's feelings were hurt?

Jack: I had no idea her feelings were hurt. I'm shocked to hear she felt that way. I was afraid the logistics of the class would make it difficult for me to pay attention to Denise and she would end up doing more standing around than teaching. It was never a question of her competence. I didn't want her to feel ignored and was trying to be thoughtful.

This is a perfect example of the Dumb Stuff that constructive candor eliminates. If Denise and Jack hadn't

discussed this incident, their wires would have been per-
manently crossed. Jack would have forever patted himself
on the back for being thoughtful. Denise would have forever felt hurt and resentful because of the slap-in-the-face
message she heard.

An isolated incident like this won't destroy a relationship. The cumulative effect will. In a dynamic relationship, silence is a deadly enemy. Constructive feedback
is a loyal friend. You wouldn't expect to be successful on
your job without input from your employer. The same
is true for your relationship. If, instead of suffering in
silence, Denise had said, "It hurts my feelings that you
don't want my help," Jack would have had the opportunity to clarify his intentions. The damage would have
been avoided. Jack would have earned Frequent Foreplay
Miles for being thoughtful. Denise would have earned
them for supporting Jack in being the responsive partner
he wants to be.

The habit of constructive candor goes beyond giving
your partner a heads-up on what's made you feel bad. It's
also about reinforcing the positive. For instance, my sweetheart Dale plays the French horn, but I attended only the
occasional concert. One day he gave me Frequent Foreplay
Miles for being in the audience. He said he liked looking
out from the stage and seeing me there. I learned that he
feels supported when I attend. So I not only go more often, I take it a step further by sending an email invitation
to our friends. I do my best to sit in his line of sight so we
can smile at each other. If he has a solo part, I give thumbs-

up to let him know how proud I am of my guy.

With Frequent Foreplay Miles you learn how to give and receive feedback that will support both of you in being the best, most responsive partners possible. You learn to identify and candidly discuss, in a common language and in a safe context, how your partner's behavior has both positively and negatively affected you. In so doing you wipe out damage from head butts, stepped-on toes, and crossed wires and, even better, prevent it from happening in the days and years ahead.

Reason #3: You learn how to turn knee jerk negative spin into positive spin.

Denise's response to Jack's effort to be thoughtful is an example of how we so often spin our sweetheart's behavior into something that is 180° from the truth. Tossing dirty gym socks on the floor may be seen by your partner as an inconsiderate gesture even though, hot and sweaty from a workout, a shower was your only thought. Leaving trash in the car may be interpreted as unappreciative when all that was on your mind was picking up the kids and getting dinner on the table. What makes negative spin so dangerous is that we too often keep it to ourselves, forming opinions—and grudges—that our partner has no ability to address or rectify.

When Jack said, "No thanks," to Denise's offer to help, she was hurt and angry because she thought—*without any evidence whatsoever*—that he didn't think she was competent to help. If she had put a positive spin on it, e.g., he didn't want to spoil her day off, his FFM balance would have gone up and she could have happily spent the day at the spa. I could go into "psychobabble" about why you hear negative messages from the person who loves you, but does it really matter? Not if you spin in a positive direction. When you can't, march right into the constructive candor we just discussed. You'll find that your partner more often than not has the best of intentions or is simply on automatic pilot, acting without conscious thought.

In the next chapter, you'll learn how using your Foreplay Back-Pocket Guide helps you turn knee jerk negative spin into positive spin. However, this benefit is best reinforced by the process of tracking because you are required to think about your interactions with your partner, analyze why you felt whatever emotion your sweetheart's behavior evoked, and look at it in the light most favorable to your sweetheart. By re-examining the "message" as well as your knee jerk reaction in the calm light of conscious analysis, you learn to substitute positive for negative spin.

Reason #4: You create and sustain a generous state of mind.

You began your relationship with generosity of spirit and perspective. You saw the best in your sweetheart, ignoring blatant faults and personality flaws, giving your new love the benefit of every doubt. As unaired and unresolved hurts and disappointments stack up, however, resentment builds and generosity declines. Newton's first law of physics states that an object in motion tends to stay in motion in the same direction unless acted upon. That's applicable here. The longer your list of gripes, the less generous you are toward your partner and the quicker you are to add to the list. If you're headed down the path of resentment, you'll keep marching in that direction—at a faster and faster pace—unless you hit the attitude brakes and make a point-of-view U-turn.

I've had to do it in my marriage. I am a nutcase about timeliness and it makes me crazy when others keep me waiting. Dale, on the other hand, is relaxed about time commitments. In the early days of our relationship, he was late often enough that my belief about him became "he is always late." My thought process went like this: *Dale is always late, which is rude. He has no respect for me or my time. He thinks his time is more valuable. That is arrogant and self-centered. Yada yada yada...* until I had myself all worked up and royally irritated so that even when he was prompt, I began our time together in a less than generous state of mind. Not good.

Here's the reality check: Dale's Foreplay Navigator on this issue is different from mine. To him, who cares about a few minutes here or there? If someone keeps him waiting, he doesn't get his shorts in a knot. He entertains himself until the doorbell rings. If it's important to catch a plane, he's there. When there's room for slide, he relaxes.

After several years of getting my own "shorts" in a knot, I decided that I needed to be more generous in the way I thought about my honey. First, I recognized that according to Dale's Foreplay Navigator, it is not mutually exclusive to be late and still have respect for me. He isn't arrogant or self-centered. He's an in-the-moment kind of guy—something I admire about him and wouldn't want to change. Then it hit me: it was arrogant and self-centered of *me* to expect him to become my clone on this issue.

Now, I don't demand perfection. I simply support Dale in being successful by letting him know when it's important that he arrive on schedule. I give him bunches of Frequent Foreplay Miles when he's on time. Because Dale has learned how important timeliness is to me, he pays more attention to the clock. He wins. I win. We're both much happier.

Frequent Foreplay Miles teaches you to focus on the positive. In doing so, you recreate and sustain the generosity of spirit and perspective that was the hallmark of your early days together.

Reason #5: You learn to embrace differences as ways to express love and strengthen your bond.

If you and your partner were identical in taste and preferences, it would be easy to pick the perfect gift—just buy exactly what you want. Since you're not twins, picking the perfect gift can present a major and sometimes frustrating challenge. But, oh boy, it's a beautiful thing when your sweetheart's eyes light up and you know you've nailed it. Spending the last five bucks in your pocket on your honey's favorite taffy when you prefer jellybeans, says, "Sweetheart, I'm putting you first." Buying your love bug a tome on

29

history that will have his nose buried for weeks instead of the legal thriller you would devour in one sitting, lets him know you've honored his preferences. That's nailing it.

Differences, large and small, provide opportunities to do those things and behave in ways that resonate with your sweetheart according to his or her Foreplay Navigator. There's no better way to express love than that. This isn't just true for gift giving. It's true for how you behave and how you interact with your partner. Let me give you an example.

Susan had a particularly bad day at work, starting with a computer crash and the resignation of her top programmer. Stan wanted to have flowers waiting for Susan when she got home. Her favorite flowers are tulips but they were out of season. So Stan found a photograph of a tulip bouquet, blew it up on his computer, printed it, pasted it to cardboard, and cut it out. The cardboard bouquet, accompanied by a sentimental note from Stan, was standing in a crystal vase where Susan would see it the minute she got home. What made this especially meaningful to the emotional Susan is that she is fond of romantic gestures while the pragmatic Stan finds them a bit silly and contrived. That goofy cardboard bouquet landed squarely within Susan's Foreplay Navigator, made her laugh, and instantly lifted her spirits. Sure, she would have appreciated any flowers. But it was Stan taking himself outside his comfort zone and doing something "so Susan" that so profoundly expressed his love she was able to let the stress of the day take a back seat to the joy of their relationship. Wow!

To hit that bull's eye Stan needed to know that Susan's favorite flower is tulip and, more importantly, that she values romantic gestures. Frequent Foreplay Miles helps you learn each other's Foreplay Navigator so you can nail it time and again.

Reason #6: You learn to honor and protect your relationship as something bigger than the two of you.

There's almost nothing worse than facing the no-win situation of resentfully giving in to your sweetheart's wishes or making your sweetie unhappy by doing what you want to do. It truly sucks when you've been given front-row tickets to the fight of the century for the same night as her grandmother's 90th birthday party. It's hard to figure out which of you will stay home and take care of your two-year old twins on the weekend of your annual girls' getaway and the golf tournament he's favored to win. And how do you decide, for example, what to do when one of you receives a job offer that requires moving to another state, away from the other's family?

I wish I could tell you that resolving no-win situations is as simple as drawing straws, but you know that's not true. What I can tell you is that if your relationship is mired down by the Dumb Stuff, these situations can easily become "do it my way to prove you love me," an opportunity to even a tit-for-tat score, or a simple power play. You may get your way, but the relationship loses.

When you are committed to each other, you create a separate entity called a "relationship." Each of you and the relationship are like the three legs of a stool. If any one of the legs breaks, the stool collapses. When you're faced with a no-win situation, you need to take you, your partner, and the strength of the relationship into account. "Winning" through sheer force of will, by cajoling, pushing, pulling, or in any way that makes the other resentful causes serious cracks in the relationship. If each of you has built up significant Frequent Foreplay Miles in advance, you are both able to approach the situation with a generous state of mind and a solid buffer of good will.

If your partner has been looking forward to his golf tournament all year, has been practicing for hours daily to take just one stroke off his handicap, competing in the tournament will give him bragging rights for the next six months, *and* he has a whole bunch of Frequent Foreplay Miles stockpiled, then making the decision to stay home (or take the twins with you) is easier, if not more pleasurable. On the other hand, if your girls' getaway is your first chance since the twins were born to take a break from unending child care, you tell your honey that one more weekend of diapers and drool and you'll be driveling and drooling yourself, *and* your Frequent Foreplay Miles balance is way up there, he's more likely to step up to the plate, take on daddy duty and send you off graciously.

It is easier to resolve these situations in favor of the relationship when you've developed the habit of constructive candor, when you have a generous state of mind, when you accept that differences in your Foreplay Navigators are not matters of right and wrong, and when your relationship is as free of the Dumb Stuff as possible. You get there with Frequent Foreplay Miles.

Reason #7: You keep new-love playfulness alive.

As you learned in Chapter 1, you can't sustain best-foot behavior indefinitely. The real you, foibles and all, eventually makes an appearance. It isn't always pretty. And sometimes you inadvertently mess up, to the annoyance (or worse!) of your sweetheart. Playfulness takes a back seat when he has to duck and take cover during your PMS tirade… or she has to put up with your road rage… or you lose your temper when the kids redecorate the living room with finger paint… or she promises but forgets to pick up your good suit from the cleaners and you have the most important meeting of your life the next morning… or he helps himself to a piece of the cake you made for your kindergartner's school bake sale… or when any one of the bazillion annoying things that can happen does.

What's more, the mind-numbing fatigue that comes with everyday life has a way of squelching playfulness. When you were jacked up on new-love hormones, you could shrug off the week from hell, strap on your dancing shoes, and let the good times roll. But now, when what used to be date night arrives, you find yourselves on the couch in your sweats, sharing delivery pizza and watching a Netflix DVD. Instead of lounging in bed after Saturday morning sex, you get a head start on weekend errands. It's easy to slip into the rut you said you'd never fall into. Fortunately, climbing out of the rut doesn't require major planning or an expensive night on the town. My friend Dave got a ton of Frequent Foreplay Miles when, one Saturday night, he turned off the TV, pulled the game Twister from where he had hidden it under the sofa, and challenged his wife Michelle. Two guesses where that led! They didn't get out of bed until noon the next day.

Frequent Foreplay Miles encourages and rewards "best foot" behavior. It's easier to be playful when everyone is behaving in ways that encourage love and intimacy. Frequent Foreplay Miles helps keep your relationship more like it was in the beginning, when playfulness came naturally and easily. And, when your sweetheart does something over-the-top wonderful that reminds you why you fell in love in the first place, you'll be inspired to reciprocate with a car wash, a me-day at the spa, a trip to the bedroom, a surprise weekend in Paris, or whatever your version of stepping out of the rut may be.

Reason #8: You will experience personal growth.

Your subtler Foreplay Navigator points are imbedded in your subconscious so deeply you're unaware of them. (I'll be discussing this in greater depth in the next chapter.) What you don't know you can't communicate or control. Frequent Foreplay Miles makes you more aware of the things that affect your relationship, including *your* patterns of behavior, *your* intentions, and *your* expectations. For example, if you find that you consistently dock your sweetheart for things that make you feel unloved, maybe the problem isn't your partner's behavior. Maybe it's your self-image.

Frequent Foreplay Miles enables you to identify what's not working for you. Is it your partner's behavior? Or, is it your own issue that needs attention? The more developed you are as an individual, the better partner you will be.

It's not always easy to understand why we hear negative messages or why something is particularly important to us. It took me a long time to understand that I'm neurotically fastidious about my material things because they are the visible evidence of a level of success I never expected to achieve. All I knew was that it chapped my hide when Dale used a dining room chair as a ladder or an expensive watering can to change the oil in his car.

To Dale, things are to be used in whatever way is expedient at the moment. The accumulation of things is not important to him. To me, my beautiful home is a reminder that I overcame many hurdles to be successful. As a result, I take care of my things. This realization and my ability to communicate it to Dale made him understand why I get cranky when, to my way of thinking, my stuff is being abused. Although I didn't stop taking care of my things, I stopped having a heart attack over a small scratch or a hissy fit over a dining room chair turned ladder.

Frequent Foreplay Miles helps you better see and know yourself. You can more completely share with your partner. And, you can make changes in those things that may be getting in the way of a great relationship or are not serving you.

Reason #9: You learn to deal with habits that might otherwise drive each other crazy.

Let's face it. You're not going to become a clone of your sweetheart no matter how many Frequent Foreplay Miles are up for grabs. As wonderful as you may be—and I don't doubt that you are—you came hardwired with certain habits and traits that you cannot change and are going to drive your partner crazy. For example, Dale is forgetful. He can no more change that about himself than he can change his eye color from hazel to blue.

It's not as though I'm perfect. I have a terrible habit of anticipating what other people are going to say and saying it for them. I know it's rude and I try not to do it, but I too often forget. This habit extends to stepping on Dale's punch line. He is a great storyteller and it drives him bananas when I jump in before he's done.

Dale is a little more casual around me with certain body functions than I would prefer. No matter how often I tell him it's not cute, he remains unconvinced. I'm a little too bossy and fussy for Dale's taste. He's a little too relaxed and messy for mine.

Despite these annoying habits, we get along just fine because we pay attention to accumulating Frequent Foreplay Miles. That, as you've already learned, inspires generosity and keeps you focused on the positive. The secret to getting away with habits that make your partner nuts is keeping a whopping big FFM balance. And remember this: for every time you grit your teeth or roll your eyes over something your partner says or does, your partner does the same thing about you. Want your partner to be generous? Be the same.

Reason #10: You more easily cope with in-laws, children, friends, and other "fellow travelers."

In a paraphrase of John Donne, no relationship is an island, entire unto itself. You each come to the relationship with your own Foreplay Navigator in hand and an entire cadre of people, some you'd like to leave behind but can't (like your brother-in-law) and some you can't live without (like children or BFF). Your sweetie comes with the same gear in tow. Only if you're lottery-winning lucky will you love and enjoy all of your sweetheart's VIPs. At least one of them is likely to bring out your homicidal tendencies. Ditto for your partner. Negotiating those various relationships in a way that doesn't adversely affect your primary relationship takes skill, patience, understanding, and sometimes just sheer will power. Staying focused on earning and not losing Frequent Foreplay Miles makes it easier.

Your sweetheart is the most important person in your love life. Others, especially children, play an equally—but different—important role. There will be times when your sweetheart's other relationships must take precedence over his or her relationship with you. A sick child or parent, a friend in the midst of a divorce, a crisis at the office, even a sick pet, will demand immediate attention. The demands of other relationships may put your partner in a rotten mood, often taken out on you as the only available punching bag. It may not be fair but it's the role a sweetheart sometimes plays. Doing it lovingly is a great way to garner Frequent Foreplay Miles.

Accepting and understanding that your sweetheart is pulled in multiple directions is easier when you focus on earning Frequent Foreplay Miles. And, remember, when you keep a high balance yourself, your partner will always feel more generous toward you, making it easier to juggle your own competing demands.

Do the intelligent thing.

Knowing what you know now, what's the intelligent thing to do? That's right. Make Frequent Foreplay Miles, both the philosophy and the process, part of your relationship right now. And while you're at it, use every opportunity to earn Frequent Foreplay Miles or to add them to your sweetheart's account.

Because we want our frequent flyer miles to grow, Dale and I fly American Airlines when we travel. We use an affinity credit card for all purchases, earning a mile for each dollar we charge. The big hits come from flight awards and large purchases, including the car we once charged. We don't fly every day and we certainly don't buy a car every day, but we buy groceries, gas or make other small purchases daily, all on our affinity credit card. By paying attention to accumulating frequent flier miles, we've flown free to Denmark, Chile, Peru, Hawaii, and other fabulous places.

Likewise, your Frequent Foreplay Miles add up quickly when you remember the power of small daily kindnesses. You notice she's running late so you clean her cat's litter box even though the cat won't give you the time of day. Or you sew a button on his shirt although he knows where the needle and thread are kept as well as you do. If you start every day by asking yourself how you can make your sweetheart's day a little easier, nicer, or better, your Frequent Foreplay Miles balance will be in the stratosphere before you know it.

Never miss an opportunity to go for the gold. She doesn't earn her PhD every day. Make it special. He doesn't get a promotion every day. Celebrate it. Take a page out of Steve's book. My clients Erin and Steve thought their estate plan was done. Wrong. The "whoops!" child made his appearance 12 years after the last one. When they visited my office to add the little guy to their will, they brought pictures. In one of the photos Erin was in the hospital bed, holding the new baby, surrounded by dozens of roses. I ooh'ed and aah'ed over the baby, then commented on the flowers. While Steve blushed a bright (but very pleased) red, Erin explained they had so little money when the first three were born, Steve couldn't afford flowers. Things had improved by the time the whoops! child showed up. Steve had four dozen roses delivered to Erin's room, one for each of their four children. Erin was so touched she cried for days. A sweet husband, four-dozen roses, and new-baby hormones make for lots of happy tears—and lots of Frequent Foreplay Miles.

Daily acts of small kindness really add up, especially those that land squarely in your sweetheart's Foreplay Navigator.

You can fly solo.

You get the best results from this book when both partners read each chapter, participate in the chapter exercises, and do the tracking. But if your sweetheart isn't interested, don't worry. You can reap the benefits of Frequent Foreplay Miles even if you fly solo. Here's why.

- *Generosity begets generosity.* The more generous you are in bestowing Frequent Foreplay Miles, the more naturally generous your sweetheart will be.

- *Improved behavior inspires improved behavior.* The quickest way to change someone's behavior is to change your own. The more you focus on accumulating Frequent Foreplay Miles, the more responsive a partner you will be. Fulfilling your sweetheart's needs will inspire your partner to do the same for you.

- *Observing your sweetheart's behavior is almost as good as hearing it straight from the horse's mouth.* While direct input from your sweetheart is best, after reading this book you will have an enhanced ability to take cues from your sweetie's behavior. If your sweetheart gets weepy over Hallmark card commercials, she is sentimental about important days. The smart partner would take this information and use it to pick up Frequent Foreplay Miles on the anniversary of their first date.

- *You'll experience personal growth to the betterment of the relationship.* With Frequent Foreplay Miles you'll learn more about yourself and your own Foreplay Navigator. You'll be able to change those things that aren't working. And, as an added benefit, you'll become a better person to everyone in your life.

If you accumulate Frequent Foreplay Miles with the same enthusiasm and dedication that a traveler collects frequent flyer miles, your relationship will thrive and bring you more joy than you ever imagined.

*3

Foreplay Back-Pocket Guide:
Avoiding Turbulence

> *I used to believe that marriage would diminish me, reduce my options, that you had to be someone less to live with someone else when, of course, you have to be someone more.*
>
> —Candice Bergen

Now that you know how Frequent Foreplay Miles will enhance your relationship bliss, you're no doubt hoping I'll give you an easy-to-follow rulebook. Wouldn't it be great if you could turn to the "Date Night" section and see that taking her out to dinner at a jacket-required restaurant is worth 200 more Frequent Foreplay Miles than taking her to the local BBQ joint? Or you could turn to the "Redeem Miles" section to determine if bringing home three kittens is worth the HUGE Frequent Foreplay Miles deduction he'd give you?

Come on. You know it's not that simple. If I could give you a rulebook that covered every foreplay situation you'll ever face, I'd be a wealthy girl indeed. As much as you and I wish otherwise, I can't. What I can do is give you a back-pocket guide to whip out as needed. That guide consists of four simple questions to help you do an on-the-spot Frequent Foreplay Miles analysis of any situation. Get in the habit of consciously and consistently referencing your Guide until it becomes second nature. This will help you avoid knee jerk (emphasis on the jerk) reactions, be more keenly aware of your Foreplay Navigator and that of your sweetie, and get it right time and again. To help you quickly reference your Guide, remember the acronym LAND— Lock, Ace, Navigate, Do. I've highlighted the words of what should become your mantra so you can make a perfect three-point landing in every situation.

The four questions are:

1. How can I **LOCK** in Frequent Foreplay Miles?

2. How can I help my sweetheart **ACE** Frequent Foreplay Miles?

3. How can I **NAVIGATE** from negative to positive spin?

4. What can I **DO** so we both get Frequent Foreplay Miles?

The only rule is, "It depends."

Let's take a closer look at why you need to keep your Foreplay Back-Pocket Guide™ handy and how it works in everyday life. Go to any airline's website and you'll find a complete set of rules for their frequent flyer program. It's easy for an airline to have rules: it doesn't give a rat's behind whether you fly for business or personal reasons, what book you read on the flight, who you travel with, or what you wear. When it comes to Frequent Foreplay Miles, however, there can be no published rules because awards and withdrawals depend on the circumstances at that moment.

Need an example? Let's take my personal pet peeve: being late. In a vacuum, being late is just, well, being late. But let's compare different circumstances and you tell me which will result in the biggest FFM deduction.

Marion is dressed for the party and waiting for Harry to pick her up. He is an hour late because:

A. He didn't allow enough time for traffic.

B. He stopped to have a beer with a buddy.

C. He detoured by his ex-wife's house to jump start her dead battery.

If you're like most people, you immediately picked C. Let's take a closer look. B and C are pretty much equal. In both, Harry put somebody ahead of his sweetheart—always a losing proposition. If Marion thinks Harry's buddy is a jerk and his ex-wife is quite nice, B will cost Harry the most. B may also cost Harry if he has an alcohol problem. And C...well, if Harry's ex has a dead battery, she really ought to be calling AAA.

Even that analysis isn't the end of the story. There are other considerations.

Marion's Foreplay Navigator. How much does Marion care if Harry is late? It may be the thing that pushes her buttons. Then again, she may shrug it off and use the extra time to balance her checkbook. Does it make a difference if he calls to let her know he'll be late? How much does Marion care whether Harry has a friendship with his ex?

The Circumstances. Does Harry know, or are the circumstances such that he should know, being on time for this particular event is important to Marion? If Marion has an appetizer tray to contribute to the party, she may want to arrive early. Perhaps she's a co-hostess and needs to be there to greet guests. If Harry messes this up, he'll lose Frequent Foreplay Miles no matter how lax Marion might otherwise be about the issue of timeliness.

Harry's Frequent Foreplay Miles Balance. The higher Harry's balance, the less likely Marion is to ding him. Even if she does, it will be for fewer FFM than if his account balance is low. Why? Because the more Frequent Foreplay Miles you have, the happier (and, therefore, the more generous) your sweetheart will be. The lower your balance, the more likely your sweetheart is to make a deduction and the bigger it will be.

This is where your handy-dandy Foreplay Back-Pocket Guide can save your life—or at least your intimacy—if you keep it close at hand. To help you, we'll take a look at examples of how using the Guide plays out in real life. Before we do, let's examine how flying on autopilot can affect your relationship.

Watch out for mid-air collisions!

"Flying on autopilot" is when you act and react without conscious reference to your own Foreplay Navigator. When it comes to day-to-day interactions with your partner, let alone uh-oh dicey situations, flying on autopilot can get you into serious trouble and lead to countless misunderstandings. Here's why:

A Foreplay Navigator is a whole lot more than a book of black-and-white rules, preferences, and opinions that can be clearly articulated. You wouldn't need this or any other book to help you have a great relationship if it were as simple as:

- Knowing that your sweetheart prefers an Almond Joy to a Snickers, would never wear a sweater with an embroidered designer logo no matter how cool the sweater may be, thinks Steve Martin is the funniest comedian alive, eats meatloaf with ketchup, values neatness above all other virtues, goes weak-kneed over Siamese kittens, would rather ride a bike than drive, thinks walks in the rain are romantic, and loves Sudoku but wouldn't waste a minute on a crossword puzzle; and

- Letting your sweetie know that you like blue better than green, hate plaid, are a dog person, prefer a sports car to an SUV, expect flowers on your anniversary, love jazz, will never in a-million-years-so-don't-bother-to-ask attend the rodeo, get nauseous at the mere thought of eggplant but can't resist rocky road ice cream, rank Bill Murray as the most brilliant actor ever born, and adore Beethoven but think Mozart is overrated.

Likes, dislikes and opinions are easy to articulate and knowing your sweetie's certainly makes it easier to rack up Frequent Foreplay Miles. But your Foreplay Navigator is a complex matrix of everything that makes you tick, think what you think, and behave as you behave. Much of it is so deeply embedded in your subconscious and so ingrained at the cellular level you aren't even aware of it and surely can't articulate it.

Your Foreplay Navigator includes perceptions and beliefs that to you are so obviously right as to be tantamount to a "universal truth" that automatically guides you and need never be consciously referenced. We acknowledge that our sweetheart has likes, opinions, and points of view that differ from our own. We too often, however, mistakenly assume that our partner is guided by the same "universal truth." Here's an example:

Diana and Jordan met at a cooking class for vegetarians. Diana is a vegetarian on moral grounds and believes it is wrong to kill any living thing. One evening, shortly after they began dating, the two were cuddled on the couch watching a movie when they spotted a spider climbing the wall. Diana got up to fetch a container so she could capture and release the little guy. She was horrified when Jordan casually tossed a tennis shoe at and squished what to Diana was God's precious eight-legged creation. Jordan raised a victory fist and proclaimed the world to be a better place with one less icky spider. In that moment Diana discovered that her "universal truth" wasn't so universal after all. Jordan is a vegetarian for health reasons. It hadn't occurred to Diana to ask Jordan why he was a vegetarian. She assumed he thought as she did because, after all, her point of view was so obviously right! This clash of Foreplay Navigators sparked a heated "butt heads" argument over who was "right" and who was "wrong" about the sacredness of arachnid life. Jordan was never persuaded to Diana's point of view, but because he adored her, he agreed to never again squish a bug.

Self-perception is often a belief-turned-universal-truth. Perhaps you have concluded that you are just a bit unlovable, not so smart, more homely than pretty or handsome, untalented, clumsy, inarticulate, or suffering from any other "disability" that messes with self-confidence and a healthy ego. When you have beliefs about yourself that diminish your self-value (and who doesn't), it's easy to see and hear negative messages when no such thing is intended. That's

49

why when your sweetheart points out the word you mis-spelled, you worry that he or she thinks you're stupid. Or when your partner forgets to call as promised, you question the sincerity of his or her affection. Or when your sweet-heart admires a member of the opposite sex, you fear he or she has one foot out the door.

For reasons I'll never quite understand, we are pro-grammed to quickly believe the worst about ourselves and pooh-pooh the rest. If a complete stranger walks up to you and says, "You're ugly," you're more likely to immediately schedule a makeover, if not an appointment with a plastic surgeon, than you are to think that the stranger wouldn't know beautiful if it slapped him in the face. On the other hand, if the stranger says, "You're beautiful," you'll either say out loud or think that the guy must be blind not to no-tice that your chin's too big, your forehead is too high, your eyes are too close together, your nose is too big, or your hair is too stringy, for you to ever be considered beautiful. This programming, combined with "universal truth" about our value (or lack thereof), is what makes it easy to hear and, even worse, believe negative messages never intended by your partner. For that reason, it is critical that you learn to spin your sweetheart's words and actions in a positive light to avoid the grudges and resentment that get in the way of having a great, Totally Intimate relationship.

Your Foreplay Navigator includes attributes that de-fine you as a person. On the plus side, that's the stuff that makes you adorable—the way you make people laugh, a heart so tender orphans and stray dogs are drawn to you like bees to blooms, a generous heart, an ability to inspire, empathy, a way with words, or other attributes that make you a marvelously wonderful human being. On the flip side, this may include a penchant for procrastination, a tendency to envy the success of others, a flair for dramatic overreaction, jealousy, a short fuse, excessive competitiveness, or other things that make you less than perfect—at least in the eyes of others, if not your own.

You've learned that it's a mix of your preferences, opinions, priorities, standards, points of view, and sensitivities, all shaped by DNA, upbringing, education, philosophical or religious training, life experience, culture, and self-perception that forms your personal guidance system. As you amble through your day—acting, reacting, behaving, doing what you do, and being what you are—you seldom give conscious thought or refer to your guidance system. You've got autopilot switched on. But think about this for a moment: if every pilot in the sky had the plane's navigation system on autopilot and then kicked back, midair collisions would occur right and left. We humans are on autopilot most of the time—which may explain a lot about the state of human affairs! From a relationship point of view, however, if both you and your sweetheart are flying on autopilot, collisions that destroy intimacy will occur with regularity. **Your Foreplay Back-Pocket Guide helps you turn autopilot off so you can be more keenly aware of your own Foreplay Navigator and that of your sweetheart.**

In the following examples, the "right outcome" will be obvious. That's because hindsight is always 20/20. However, all but the last is a true-life example of how somebody got it wrong; the last is an example of getting it right. As we go through the examples, think of situations where you got it wrong and how things would have turned out differently if you had owned and used a Foreplay Back-Pocket Guide. Okay, here we go . . .

Question #1: How can I LOCK in Frequent Foreplay Miles?

Julie and Rod have been married for two years. Rod has an extended family with which he is very close. Large family gatherings are common. Rod was married to Claire for 22 years before marrying Julie, and his family members often mindlessly refer to Julie as Claire. While driving to such a gathering, Julie says to Rod, "I have to, and do, remember all your family's names. Why can't they remember just one name: mine?"

If Rod asks himself question #1—"How can I **LOCK** in Frequent Foreplay Miles?"—what will he do?

- Rod will remind Julie that his family means no ill will and it's silly to let it bother her or to take it so personally.

- Rod will promise to speak to the worst offenders and ask them to be more mindful of Julie's name.

You're probably thinking, "Duh! Number 2, Dude."

You're right. In hindsight, that's the obviously appropriate course of action. At the moment when Julie made the comment, however, here's what happened:

Julie: *You know, Rod, I have to, and I do, remember every one of your family members' names. Why can't they remember just one? Mine."*

Rod: *Come on, Julie, you know they don't mean any harm. They all love you. Why do you take it so personally?*

Julie: *If they love me so much, why can't they remember my name? What I don't understand is why you don't care that they're inconsiderate. I feel like you're more worried about offending your family than you care about my feelings.*

Rod: *Of course I care about your feelings. I just don't think it's such a big deal.*

Julie: *It's a big deal to me.*

Rod: *You're being silly and should get over it.*

Julie goes silent. For the rest of the evening.

Rod was on autopilot, reacting to his dread of confrontation instead of responding to Julie's needs. When Julie finally spoke again, it was to tell Rod that he made her feel unimportant by discounting her feelings. If Rod had taken a moment to ask question #1, there's a darned good chance he would have sucked it up and asked his family to be more careful. Julie would have felt loved, protected, and respected. Rod would have earned a truckload of Frequent Foreplay Miles and, for the cherry on top he'd feel good about successfully facing down his fear of confrontation. The evening ended with the two of them sleepless, back-to-back with a wall of ice between them. It could have ended with sweet lovin'.

Here's another example. Sally suggested and George agreed that they should celebrate their tenth anniversary by taking a trip to Paris. For the previous nine years the always-practical George has given Sally either a scarf or a book for every special occasion. True to form, George selected a silk scarf imprinted with French words. Sally selected a silver frame to hold George's favorite picture from Paris. She had it engraved with the date of their anniversary and their names.

When they exchanged gifts the night before their departure for France, Sally couldn't hide her disappointment that George hadn't selected a gift more special and, in her mind, more appropriate to the occasion. She snidely commented that if the picture frame weren't already engraved, she'd take it back and exchange it for a tie imprinted with the Eiffel Tower. George's feelings were hurt at Sally's unexpected reaction. After all, he had simply done what he always did.

When I heard this story, I asked George what gift he would have selected had he thought of Sally's Foreplay Navigator. After just a moment's reflection, he said paper, scrapbook, and supplies for making a memory album of Paris because Sally's hobby is scrapbooking. Sally said she would have been over-the-moon thrilled with that gift and bragged to her friends for weeks. Had George referred to his Guide and Question #1, he would have turned autopilot off, selected a gift that landed foursquare in Sally's Foreplay Navigator and, in the process, picked up oodles of Frequent Foreplay

Miles. Their trip to Paris would have started on better foot-
ing and been a more intimate experience. Every time Sally
looked at that memory album, she would have been reminded how book-and-scarf George broke the mold. Each time
she did, he'd earn a few more Frequent Foreplay Miles.

Switching autopilot to off frees your mind to analyze
the situation in a way that puts your partner first. Doing
those things that recognize and honor your partner's preferences, unique qualities, and differences is a surefire way to
pick up Frequent Foreplay Miles.

**Question #2: How can I help my sweetheart ACE
           Frequent Foreplay Miles?**

Let's revisit Rod and Julie. If, when she felt the first twinge
of irritation at being called Claire, Julie had asked herself
question #2—"How can I help my sweetheart ACE Frequent Foreplay Miles?"—which of the following choices
would she have made?

• Julie would have waited for Rod to eventually figure
  out what to do.

• Julie would have told Rod she is hurt when his
  family members call her by the wrong name and
  asked him to mention it to the worst offenders.

Again, the answer is obvious at this moment. At the
time, however, Julie was on autopilot. I asked Julie why
it had taken two years to complain. She replied, "It's so
obvious that his family is thoughtless. This 'problem' goes
back to our engagement party when Rod's uncle gave a

toast to 'Rod and Claire' instead of 'Rod and Julie.' If the situation had been reversed, I would have handled it a long, long time ago. I was disappointed in Rod. I thought he didn't care enough about my feelings to address the problem. I finally had no choice but to bring it up."

Rod was surprised to hear this. He hadn't realized Julie was offended and because he found his family's numb-headedness more amusing than rude, he hadn't perceived a problem. Her "universal truth" was that (a) one's family shouldn't call one's sweetheart by the wrong name, and (b) if they do, one should put a stop to it, and (c) if one doesn't put a stop to it, he must not care about his sweetheart's feelings. Since Rod didn't do (b), Julie spent two years harboring a grudge "justified" by (c).

Julie's two-year silence was a disservice to her, to Rod, and to their relationship. She set herself up for disappointment, set Rod up for failing to meet secret expectations, and guaranteed that the relationship would be damaged. If Julie had right away asked Question #2, she stood a far better chance of getting the end-result she wanted—two years earlier!

Likewise, Sally had enough experience with George to know he was a book-and-scarf gift-giver. Although she was usually fine with that, her Foreplay Navigator dictated that a tenth anniversary called for a stepped-up gift. When I asked Sally how she contributed to the disappointing outcome, she said, "I assumed that because George had agreed to my suggestion we celebrate in Paris he got it. I now realize that what I was really doing is crossing my fingers that he'd know what to do. I thought that if I told him what to do, it would somehow lose its emotional punch." Sally went on to admit she had joked with a friend that George would probably give her a travel book for Paris. That "joke" was her cue that George needed a helping hand out of his gift-giving rut. Had she then asked how she could make it easy for George to pick up Frequent Foreplay Miles, she would have known to lend that hand. Instead, she set George up for failure and set herself up for disappointment.

Crossing your fingers that your sweetheart will read your mind or through sheer dumb luck will get it right is about as effective as flying on autopilot. Instead of telling your mother, your best friend, your co-worker, your sibling, and total strangers what you want from your sweetheart, tell your sweetheart.

Your partner wants to be responsive to your needs, wants, and hopes. Supporting his or her success in being the best partner possible by making it easy to earn Frequent Foreplay Miles is arguably the best gift you can ever give to your sweetie—and to yourself.

Question #3: How can I NAVIGATE from negative to positive spin?

Belinda's birthday was approaching. Ken asked Belinda what size he would get if he were buying an item of clothing for her. "Well," she said, "that depends on what part of my body we're talking about." By the end of the conversation, Belinda had guessed that Ken intended to buy her a bathrobe. "Ah," she said, "that's just what I need and here's exactly what I want." She then went on to describe the white terry cloth bathrobe she'd like to have.

On the day of her birthday, Ken presented Belinda with a beautifully wrapped gift. When she opened it she nearly got whiplash. It was a bathrobe, all right, and it was exactly what she wanted but for one detail: it was neon lilac. If Belinda asks herself question #3—" How can I **NAVIGATE** from negative to positive spin?"— which conclusion will she come to?

- Ken never listens to me. He always does what he wants.

- Ken must have been disappointed that I guessed what he was giving me and wanted there to be an element of surprise. It was sweet of him to think about what I needed.

This is an example pulled from my former marriage. After I opened the box and saw the neon lilac robe, I gave my ex-husband all manner of grief for not buying what I wanted. I accused him of being insensitive to my wants and spun it as proof that he ignored my feelings. Worse, I never let it go. For years, I pointed to that robe every time I wanted to "prove" he thought of himself first. He finally told me he had been hurt by my reaction and simply wanted there to be an element of surprise in the gift.

I had so much to learn! That was nearly 30 years ago, at a time when I had yet to rewrite the self-esteem chapter of my Foreplay Navigator and deal with an upbringing that left me feeling unlovable and insecure. I had been on autopilot for so long and was so entrenched in my self-perception, that I was actually surprised to learn he didn't see it my way. If I had known then what I know now, I would have asked myself, "How can I put a positive spin on this?" If I had, there's a good chance my reaction would have been more in line with reality. I would have seen the robe (ugly as it was!) as proof my sweetheart was thoughtful, not selfish. I would not have systematically contributed to trashing the intimacy we once had.

Your sweetheart loves you. If you don't believe that, perhaps you should reconsider your relationship situation. If you do believe it, then accept that your partner acts with good, albeit sometimes misguided, intentions and occasionally forgets to switch autopilot to off. When you find yourself feeling hurt or disappointed, asking yourself Question #3 helps you see the situation in a way far more likely to be founded on reality. As a bonus, it helps you understand more about your own Foreplay Navigator so you can address and change those things that may not serve you or are keeping you from having the relationship you want.

Question #4: What can I DO so we both get Frequent Foreplay Miles?

Here's another example from my life, this time from my relationship with hubby Dale. We had been dating just a few months. We were a couple but still getting to know each other.

I got a call at my law office on a Monday morning from Dale's sister's boyfriend. After I'd answered his legal question, he said, "I'll see you Wednesday evening." I told him I didn't know anything about Wednesday so he filled me in. Dale and I were expected at his sister's house to celebrate her birthday. When I next spoke to Dale, I mentioned this conversation. Unfortunately, he had forgotten about his sister's birthday and made plans to meet his ex-wife, retrieve stock certificates from her safe deposit box, have dinner and catch up. "No problem," I told him, "I've already made plans to go to a poetry reading. I'll leave it to you to square things with your sister." I then forgot about it.

On Wednesday morning, Dale told me to enjoy the poetry reading, and explained he would be "killing two birds with one stone" by taking his ex-wife to his sister's birthday celebration. I was stunned into speechlessness. By this time in our relationship, I knew we had something special and I didn't want to mess it up. Though I had come a long way in working through the personal issues that had interfered with my previous marriage, those nasty demons of insecurity and lack of self-confidence raised their ugly heads and began whispering in my ear. I was afraid to do anything that might result in Dale caring less about me. I had learned a lot since the robe incident, however. So, after stewing about it for several hours, I told the demons to shut up, took a deep breath, and asked myself question #4—" What can I **DO** so we both get Frequent Foreplay Miles?" Which of the following did I choose?

- I suffered in silence, telling myself it was no big deal.
- I told Dale how I felt and gave him the opportunity to make another decision.

This time I got it right. By asking myself Question #4, I was able to analyze the situation with clarity. I realized I had no right to be angry or upset with Dale if he didn't know that what he planned to do was a 10 on the not-all right-with-me scale. I also realized that regardless of whether I had the right to be angry with him, I would be. Not only was that unfair to Dale, it constituted a conscious choice on my part to let the relationship be damaged. I had to speak up. With a lump in my throat, I dialed his number. The conversation went like this:

Shela: Sweetheart, I'm not comfortable with you taking your ex-wife to your sister's birthday party. We were invited as a couple.

Dale: I know, but I forgot about the party and got myself boxed into a scheduling corner because I need to get my stock certificates.

Shela: I understand. I also understand that it's not fair to be upset with you without telling you how I feel. I'm telling you so you can take that into consideration in deciding what to do.

Dale: I want to make this right. If I tell my ex she's not going with me, will you still go?

Shela: Yes, I will.

Dale: Done.

Dale earned truckloads of Frequent Foreplay Miles by immediately stepping up to the plate. I got truckloads of Frequent Foreplay Miles for not making him feel defensive and giving him the choice to do the right thing. I also got a few Frequent Foreplay Miles by letting him off the hook for being such a lunkhead in the first place!

I later came to realize, as we got to know each other better, that had the situation been reversed, Dale wouldn't have thought twice about it. Our Foreplay Navigators differ dramatically on this point. My "universal truth" is that you don't take your ex to a party no matter what the circumstances. To Dale, it was no big deal, especially since I had already made plans for the evening.

Dale would agree that we fell a little more in love with each other as a result of the way we handled this dicey situation. Most importantly, by taking the time to analyze the situation from the perspective of how Dale, our budding relationship, and I could all win, I avoided the "what-the-heck" knee jerk response that I would have always regretted.

Switch autopilot to off at the first sign of turbulence.

Flying on autopilot and conscious thinking are mutually exclusive. For the most part, it's okay to be on autopilot. No one has the time to analyze every move they make and every thought they think throughout the day. When it comes to your relationship, however, it is critical that you turn auto-pilot off at the first hint your sweetheart is feeling, or you feel, the first twinge of anger, doubt, hurt, fear, jealousy, or any other emotion that gets in the way of intimacy. Your Foreplay Back-Pocket Guide helps you do that and more.

These four questions are your best tools for building up your Frequent Foreplay Miles balance and avoiding deductions caused by "violations" of your partner's Foreplay Navigator. You'll find a wallet-sized card in the Appendix that you can cut out, laminate, and carry in your back pocket. By keeping these questions in mind, you can take almost any situation or misunderstanding and turn it into an occasion for greater closeness, clearer communication, sweeter love, and stronger ties. You will more fully realize all the benefits of Frequent Foreplay Miles—in the bedroom and beyond.

Let's review. Those four key questions—with the memory-jogging words highlighted—are:

1. How can I **LOCK** in Frequent Foreplay Miles?

2. How can I help my sweetheart **ACE** Frequent Foreplay Miles?

3. How can I **NAVIGATE** from negative to positive spin?

4. What can I **DO** so we both get Frequent Foreplay Miles?

Exercise

Think of several situations where things didn't go well. Now, think about how they might have turned out differently had you consulted your Foreplay Back-Pocket Guide. A good place to start would be Part A of the list you made at the end of Chapter 1.

*4

Frequent Foreplay Miles:

The Right Way to Keep Score

> ***How do I love thee?***
> ***Let me count the ways.***
> —Elizabeth Barrett Browning

In Chapter 2, I summed up the philosophy of Frequent Foreplay Miles like this: *You get Frequent Foreplay Miles when you fly right; you lose them when you don't. The more you have, the happier your relationship will be, so rack 'em up at every opportunity and avoid losing them whenever possible.* Getting and losing Frequent Foreplay Miles…hmmmmmm, sounds a little like scorekeeping, doesn't it? In a way, it is. And isn't scorekeeping a great big relationship no-no? Absolutely—unless you do it the right way.

Two wrongs don't make a tit-for-tat right.

Every relationship guru on the planet (including me) will tell you that tit-for-tat is death to your relationship. That's two-rights-make-a-wrong justification of your bad behavior by that of your partner. Here's how it sounds:

Joe: *Alice, I was in the garage and noticed you left potting soil all over my workbench. I don't mind if you use my bench but please don't leave dirt on it.*

Alice: *Well, sorrrrry. Now you know how it feels when you track mud in the house I try so hard to keep clean.*

Alice may be a natural born tit-for-tat scorekeeper. Then again, she may be fed up with how many times Joe has ignored her request to leave his muddy shoes at the door. Regardless, she has chosen a destructive way to deal with the situation, a way that is sometimes tempting to take. You've done it, right? Okay, I'll go first. I admit it. I've sunk to that level. It doesn't work, not even in the teensiest way. That's because tit-for-tat leads to a spiral argument that only goes one way— down hill. Here's how that sounds:

Joe: *A muddy footprint easily wiped up is hardly the same as dirt that can ruin my power tools. Floors are supposed to be walked on. They get dirty.*

Alice: *Really? Well, if you don't have respect for my floor and how hard I work to keep it clean, why should I have respect for your workbench or your power tools?!!!*

Joe: **Fine. If that's your attitude, then expect a few more muddy footprints.**

Alice: **DON'T YELL AT ME!**

Joe: **YOU YELLED FIRST!!!**

Nothing like a good tit-for-tat argument to take you right back to first grade, is there? Tit-for-tat is childish and destructive. It undermines trust and trashes intimacy.

Mother Teresa and Gandhi aside, we all keep score.

You know you're not supposed to. You try not to. But show me a partner who's never said, "I owe you one," or, "You just lost a few points," or "Don't I at least get credit for [fill in the blank]," and I'll show you a partner who's not paying attention. You may be a saint about not tit-for-tatting, but you can't help noticing if, when you butt heads, your sweetie wins more often than you do. You can't help but notice if your toes have been stepped on one too many times. You can't help but notice that your sweetheart has left dirty dishes in the sink AGAIN, has "forgotten" to call AGAIN, has publicly teased and embarrassed you AGAIN, or has otherwise disappointed you or hurt your feelings AGAIN. "Noticing" may not equal "scorekeeping" in a numerical or tit-for-tat sense, but it does equal "scorekeeping" in an on-balance sense. If I were to ask you, right now, if your sweetheart's score is to the moon, well into the black but there's room for improvement, good enough to squeak by, dipping into the red, in the tank, or subterranean, you'd be able to tell me. Humans assess by quantification. If you're making a decision about whether to leave a job, move to another state, buy a car, get a dog, or stay in a relationship, you add up the pros and cons or, said another way, calculate the pluses and minuses to determine which way the scale tips.

In a relationship, pluses are being awarded and minuses are being deducted all day long. Your sweetie brings you coffee in bed, plus 5. Morning coffee follows a night of wild sex that left you happily exhausted, 30-point bonus. You have a crazy busy day of nonstop meetings and your partner has lunch delivered to your office, 20 points. Lunch includes cheesecake, 10-point bonus. Your partner borrows your car and returns it with an empty tank, minus 10. Your sweetheart leaves a wet towel on the bed, minus 5. It's your side of the bed, 15-point penalty. It's the third time this week, 50-point penalty.

It's this kind of "scorekeeping" we can't help but do. True, we don't usually give or deduct actual points, but we give greater emotional weight to those things that most affect us. If that weren't true, a surprise Porsche in the driveway would have the same Omigosh! factor as a new toaster oven. Infidelity would land you in the same hot water as forgetting to pay the cable bill.

There are plenty of times when you know you've scored big or messed up badly. Most of the time, however, neither partner is fully aware of how, why or when he or she is winning or losing points until the score goes so far into the red that the complaining begins and it's too late to repair the damage. This is especially true when it comes to The Dumb Stuff. Worse, we keep score based upon our own Foreplay Navigator without considering that our partner's might be completely different. It's like playing a board game with two different sets of rules with neither of you knowing the other's rules. Misunderstandings, accusations of rule breaking, grudges and resentment are the inevitable result.

I've seen time and again how, in a floundering relationship, each partner can recite every misstep the other has taken as "proof" that he or she is "always" wrong about one thing or another. Yet the question, "When has your partner earned points for being right?" is often met with silence. Even after my self-imposed attitude adjustment, I can recount every time I saw red because Dale was late. But I can't recall, let alone recite, the times when he was prompt. This natural tendency to notice the negative (based on our own Foreplay Navigator) and gloss over the positive is why scorekeeping is so destructive.

Sure sounds like a Catch-22, doesn't it? On the one hand, scorekeeping trashes your relationship. On the other hand, you're hardwired to do it.

It's time to stop fighting human nature.

I say, since we're going to keep score anyway, let's do it in a way that strengthens our relationship instead of tearing it down. Here's how: make it your goal to (1) earn as many Frequent Foreplay Miles as possible, (2) avoid losing them, and (3) support your sweetheart in doing the same. With the help of your Foreplay Back-Pocket Guide, you accomplish that goal when you:

- See every situation as an opportunity for emotional foreplay.

- Practice constructive candor.

- Substitute positive spin for knee jerk negative spin.

- Generously award Frequent Foreplay Miles and be slow to deduct them.

- Honor your sweetheart's preferences and differences.

- Protect the integrity of your relationship as the third leg of the stool.

Is meeting that goal easier said than done? Well, some couples will be successful by applying the information and techniques I've given you. Most couples need a bit more help. If you are in a relationship where you find yourself envying your single friends, you are sometimes on thin ice or spend too much time in the dog house, you occasionally (or often) question whether you're with the right person, are harboring grudges or feeling resentful, then I recommend you track Frequent Foreplay Miles.

Tracking requires time and discipline, two things that in today's busy world are in short supply no matter how motivated you may be. I wouldn't dream of asking you to spend valuable time unless I was certain you'll be glad you did. Before you decide whether tracking is for you, read through the instructions. You'll discover tips and techniques that will help you more effectively implement the Frequent Foreplay Miles philosophy into your everyday life and keep score the right way.

First, let's talk about point of view and mindset.

Your partner is not a remodeling project.

Believe me, if I had a magic wand, I'd wave that sucker and turn Dale into a neat freak. I'd give him a passion for being on time, for board games (especially Scrabble), and for gardening—the last because I don't garden but somebody needs to do it. I don't have a magic wand and thank goodness Dale doesn't have one! Neither do you. You might be successful in remodeling your partner if you cajole, push, prod, and manipulate, but remember the cost. You risk creating a resentful partner and possibly changing your partner into someone you no longer recognize or no longer like. There's no point in winning the battle if you lose the war.

Consider Nick and Beth:

The first week they did the Tracker, Beth gave Nick multiple deductions for his lack of neatness, including:

- Failure to put the ketchup bottle back in its assigned place in the refrigerator.

- Leaving his wallet and car keys on the kitchen table.

- Kicking his shoes off and leaving them in the front hallway.

- Draping his wet towel over the shower stall.

- Tossing his mail on the kitchen counter.

With each entry, Beth wrote that Nick's actions made her feel unappreciated for how hard she works to provide a beautiful home for their family. I met with Beth and Nick separately to help them prepare for their first tracker discussion. My conversation with Beth went like this:

Shela: Beth, I notice a consistent theme. You've given Nick quite a few dings for basically the same thing. Looks like messiness is a pet peeve of yours, is that right?

Beth: Absolutely. I work hard to keep a neat house and it irritates me no end when Nick leaves his stuff lying around.

Shela: What about the ketchup bottle?

Beth: I have a lot to do to take care of the kids and the house. I don't have time to look for things so I like them in their proper place.

Shela: Let me guess. You and Nick squabble about this.

Beth: *All the time. Nick says it's his house, too. I agree, but I'm the one primarily responsible for taking care of the house. I think I should have the final say in how that's done. Sometimes I think he leaves a mess just to make a point. I was glad when Nick agreed to tracking. Maybe I'll finally get through to him.*

Shela: *What does that mean, "getting through to him?"*

Beth: *That he'll see it my way.*

I asked Beth if she could truthfully say she was giving feedback to Nick that was unqualifiedly constructive. Was she giving him new, useful information? Or was she holding an emotional gun to Nick's head? Was she using Frequent Foreplay Miles as a way to manipulate Nick into being her clone on neatness? I sat quietly, waiting for her answer. The light bulb clicked on. Beth asked if I thought it would be more effective to give Nick Frequent Foreplay Miles when he did his part to keep the house neat. I did. I then asked Beth if it was possible she was a tad rigid in her standards. Yes, she agreed (albeit somewhat reluctantly) it was.

Tracking helped Beth change her point of view so she could see what Nick did "right" instead of what he did "wrong." She decided to relax her standard of perfection. She understood that she and Nick had differing Foreplay Navigators on this issue and that she had no greater right to have it her way than he did to have it his way. By holstering the emotional gun and acknowledging Nick for what he did right, she put an end to the squabbling that was destructive to their relationship and their intimacy.

Frequent Foreplay Miles is designed to help you support your sweetheart in being the responsive partner he or she wants to be. It is not designed to help you re-model your partner into your image of perfection. If you have the right mindset when you give feedback to your partner—whether through tracking or on the spot—there's a good chance your partner will voluntarily and happily change those things that aren't working so well. Stay focused on fixing what in yourself needs fixing and on changing what you need to change. Let your partner do the same.

Tracking: the Forms

The forms you need to track Frequent Foreplay Miles are found in the appendix. You may photocopy them or you may download easier-to-use PDF versions from my website at www.FrequentForeplayMiles.com. The forms you will use are Generosity Generator, Frequent Foreplay Miles Tracker, Tip Sheet, and Award Certificate.

Here are step-by-step instructions:

Step 1: Complete your Generosity Generator

The Generosity Generator consists of six lead-in statements that you will complete. I encourage every reader—whether you track or not—to take this feel-good generosity-building step. For those who track, the Generosity Generator establishes a beginning balance of 600 Frequent Foreplay

FFM Tip:

If your partner isn't interested in tracking, do it alone. You'll learn how to give constructive feedback, how to turn negative spin into positive spin, and more about your own Foreplay Navigator.

Miles for each of you. Because now is the time to let go of grudges and begin to develop a generous state of mind, you will only award Frequent Foreplay Miles. You will make no deductions. I encourage you to give more than one example for each statement but the total Frequent Foreplay Miles awarded will be 100 for each of the six statements regardless of how many examples you give.

To complete the statements, go back as far in time as required but don't try too hard. Just let your mind go where it goes. Let yourself again feel and savor the positive emotions that each moment you'll describe evoked. The moment need not be earth shattering or the stuff of an epic romance novel, just special to you. Here's an example from my Generosity Generator:

One of my favorite memories is the day Dale and I played hooky from work and drove to the California Coast. We spontaneously ran toward each other from opposite ends of a small deserted beach with arms outstretched. We met in the middle, embraced, and fell onto the sand laughing and kissing.

To complete the Generosity Generator:

- Photocopy or download one Generosity Generator for each partner.

- Set a time when you will exchange and discuss them. Give yourselves plenty of time to reflect on and complete the forms but no more than a week.

- Agree on a reward for completing your Generosity Generators. It doesn't matter whether it's a romantic dinner or a 50-mile bike ride so long as it's something you both enjoy and can be done within a day or two after completing the forms. Make it fun.

- Complete your forms, each of you doing so privately.

- Meet at the agreed upon time and exchange forms. Discuss them as much as feels necessary.

- Have that romantic dinner, take that 50-mile bike

FFM Tip:

When you are at your wit's end, on the ragged edge of fed up with your partner, or feeling more homicidal than charitable—even if just for the moment—take a deep breath and revisit your favorite memories. Even when you're at your happiest, revisit those memories for the sheer joy of it. Doing so will help you sustain the generosity of spirit necessary for a Totally Intimate relationship.

ride, or do whatever fun thing you picked as your reward.

Step 2: Frequent Foreplay Miles Tracker

Each partner will keep his or her own Tracker for a week. You will record any of your partner's behavior that evokes an emotion in you. You will also maintain your sweetheart's Frequent Foreplay Miles account balance. The number of Frequent Foreplay Miles awarded or deducted is determined by the emotion you felt. Feel free to modify my list so it works best for you by adding emotions and corresponding Frequent Foreplay Miles values.

A complete entry will include:

- A brief description of the behavior.
- A one-word description of the emotion the behavior evoked.

Emotion	Frequent Foreplay Miles
Ecstatic	100
Overjoyed	90
Supported	80
Thrilled	75
Delighted	60
Happy	50
Grateful	45
Proud	40
Pleased	35
Touched	30
Annoyed	-25
Irritated	-30
Aggravated	-35
Angry	-45
Hurt	-55
Disappointed	-65
Furious	-75
Brokenhearted	-85
Homicidal	-90
Devastated	-100

- A description of why the behavior generated the emotion.

- The amount of Frequent Foreplay Miles that corresponds with the emotion.

- An optional bonus or penalty based on your discretion.

- If a bonus or penalty was given, an explanation why.

Here's one of my tracker entries.

Behavior: *Dale bought me a legal thriller to read on the airplane when I was traveling alone.*

Emotion: *Grateful*

Description: *It was very thoughtful because Dale knows I'm a nervous flyer and if I were engrossed in a legal thriller (which is my favorite reading) I would be distracted from my nervousness. I felt loved and protected and was especially grateful that my flight wasn't so bad after all!*

Frequent Foreplay Miles Award: *45*

Bonus: *15*

Explanation of Bonus: *When we fly, I usually have Dale's hand to hold as comfort. I was especially touched that he realized I would be more nervous without him by my side and that he, therefore, did his best to find another way to help me through the flight.*

To complete your Trackers:

- Photocopy or download one Tracker for each partner.

- Enter a beginning balance of 600 Frequent Foreplay Miles for each of you. This is the balance carried forward from your Generosity Generator and gets you both started with an equal balance.

- Set a date for your first Tracker discussion no less than seven, but no more than ten days later. Allow sufficient time to fully discuss them. I suggest no less than an hour.

- Agree on something to do after the discussion such as a candlelit meal or sitting on the back porch holding hands. Make it something that involves more than being in the same place at the same time. Watching your favorite TV show doesn't count unless you agree to snuggle throughout the whole program and make-out during the commercials!

- Make daily entries of those things your partner says or does that evoke an emotion, even if the emotion is slight and temporary—you'll learn from all of them. You must give your partner at least one award of Frequent Foreplay Miles every day. Give Frequent Foreplay Miles when your partner does

FFM Tip:

Look for ways to give FFM to your sweetheart. Award Frequent Foreplay Miles when the wet towel—often left on the bathroom floor—ends up in the hamper. Reinforce the positive!

right what you think he or she often does "wrong." Make all entries both constructive and instructive. Refrain from using derogatory language and name-calling. Do not talk about any Tracker entry until the agreed upon time. This will help you avoid arguments from knee-jerk reactions.

Step 3: Prepare for your Tracker discussion.

This is one of the most critical steps in the process. All entries will provide information you need to be constructively candid with your sweetheart, identify what's truly important to you, and discern whether you have expectations that are undermining rather than supporting your partner and the relationship. Each entry will fall into one of two categories:

- *Instructive to your sweetheart.* These are constructive entries that will help you share your Foreplay Navigator with your sweetheart so he or she can be a more responsive partner.

- *Instructive to you.* These are entries that help you learn more about your own Foreplay Navigator, patterns of behavior, personality traits, etc.

Examine each entry you've made in your Tracker and ask yourself these questions:

- *Am I absolutely certain I made this entry with the intention of supporting my partner in being the best partner possible?* If the answer is an unqualified yes, mark it as one that is instructive to your partner; otherwise mark is as instructive to you.

- If the entry is a deduction, ask this question: *Is it possible to spin it so my sweetheart does not lose Frequent Foreplay Miles?* If so, spin it that way and either cross it out or award Frequent Foreplay Miles instead of deducting them.

- With regard to the entries that are marked as instructive to you, ask yourself if they suggest a pattern that says, "Hey, this is my problem." Think about what the entry tells you about yourself and what you may consider changing. I understand that self-analysis isn't easy. Like any new habit or skill you're trying to develop, you'll get better and better the more you roll up your sleeves and, as the Nike slogan goes, just do it.

- From the entries that are marked as instructive to your partner, select no more than ten of those to discuss with your sweetheart.

FFM Tip:

Before you lash out or give your sweetheart a piece of your mind, ask yourself if what you're about to say is unqualifiedly constructive. If not, keep it zipped until you've cooled down. Then, rephrase what you want to say so it's constructive. Or, when you have a quiet moment, think about what you can learn about yourself from the reaction you had to whatever had you bent out of shape.

FFM Tip:

Always, always, always give your sweetheart's behavior a positive spin if at all possible.
If you just can't, no matter how fast and furiously you spin, then march right into constructive candor. Help your partner be the responsive partner he or she wants to be. It's the best gift you'll ever give yourself!

Step 4: Exchange and discuss your Trackers.

Okay, for some people this will be the hard part. It might feel awkward at first but you'll get used to it.

- Take turns, with one of you discussing one of your Tracker Entries, and then the other of you discussing one of his or her entries, until you are done.

- Discuss the awards first. Read your entry out loud to your partner and elaborate as much as feels appropriate. Express gratitude for your partner and for whatever he or she did to earn the Frequent Foreplay Miles you've awarded. As the award recipient, do not quibble about whether you should have received more Frequent Foreplay Miles than your partner gave you! Accept the award graciously and with gratitude for your sweetheart's generosity.

- When you've reached the end of the awards, enjoy a long kiss. It doesn't have to be a passionate kiss that takes you to the bedroom (but if it does, don't worry about it, you can come back to the discussion later!) Make it a kiss that establishes a physical and emotional connection so you're in the right frame of mind for discussing the deductions. You'll know you're there when you feel the first tingling of an urge to get naked!

- Discuss the deductions, again taking turns. If it is your entry, read it aloud and elaborate as appropriate but be mindful that you don't belabor the point or "pile on." Avoid being accusatory and making your partner defensive. View deductions not as punitive but as ways to learn and grow in the relationship. This goes for both of you. The partner who got the deduction should be allowed to explain his or her behavior WITHOUT interruption. The partner who gave the deduction should listen with a generous state of mind and be willing to accept explanations at face value. This is not a time to make excuses for bad behavior. It is a time to accept responsibility

FFM Tip:

No matter how constructive and candid your feedback may be, it won't be heard if delivered at high decibel. It won't be received if hurled with anger and accusation. How you deliver the information is as important as the information itself.

and apologize when it's appropriate to do so. This is NOT a time to argue about who's right and who's wrong. Tracker discussions are not gripe and bitch sessions. Don't be on autopilot. Ask yourself, BEFORE you speak, if the shoe were on the other foot would you find what you're about to say helpful and constructive.

- Ask as many questions as are needed to fully understand each entry before moving to the next but don't, as they say, beat a dead horse. If you find yourselves being repetitive or argumentative, move on.

- Resolve differences whenever possible. Look for ways to turn deductions into future awards. Remember how Dale and I resolved the problem of my thumbing through the mail while he spoke? If you are unable to resolve differences, stop the discussion about that entry before it turns into an argument, and move to

FFM Tip:

A deduction isn't a penalty. It's a gift of the information that will help you be successful in the relationship. Thank your lucky stars that your sweetheart chose constructive candor over a grudge that would someday ferociously bite you on the butt when you least expect it!

the next one. It is NOT necessary that you come to agreement about each entry. It is necessary that you agree to sometimes disagree.

- Point out behavior you thought should have earned Frequent Foreplay Miles but was missed by your partner. This is the time to toot your own horn!

Step 5: Repeat Steps 2, 3 and 4.

Do weekly Trackers until you are comfortable being constructively candid and are in the habit of putting a positive spin on your partner's behavior. When you start a new Tracker, carry your balance forward from the previous Tracker.

Step Whenever: Complete and deliver the Frequent Foreplay Miles Tip Sheet.

Got an event coming up and you have specific hopes or expectations of your sweetheart? Are you worried he'll do his famous Funky Chicken at your cousin's wedding? Got your eye on a tool collection and want to head her in that direction when she goes birthday shopping? Don't risk disappointment. And, do not—it bears repeating—DO NOT rely on hints or mental telepathy! Help your sweetheart do the right thing. Give a heads up with a Frequent Foreplay Miles Tip Sheet.

Another Step Whenever: Give an Instant Award Certificate for exceptional behavior.

Did your sweetheart do something so outrageously wonderful or so beyond fantastic you're about to burst from the joy of it all? Give your partner an instant award of Frequent Foreplay Miles to cash in for something special, whether it's a car wash, a massage, or a trip to the bedroom. Okay, I know you think that only people under the age of eight give coupons, but, hey, the idea is to have fun with this. So, have fun!

Another Step Whenever: Add your own nuances.

Feel free to shape this process in any way that's better for you. Be creative. Give awards for achieving a certain Frequent Foreplay Miles balance. Relax. Have fun. It doesn't have to be hard work.

Step Always: Stay focused on the right things.

It's not your Frequent Foreplay Miles account balance that matters. Keeping score by tracking Frequent Foreplay Miles is just the fun wrapper for a serious process. What matters is that you identify the emotion you feel when your partner does this or that, know why you felt it, and have a way to deal with it. So…why do you track Frequent Foreplay Miles? Because tracking helps you on the road to Total Intimacy as you:

- See and use every occasion as an opportunity for emotional foreplay.

- Develop the habit of constructive candor.

- Turn knee jerk negative spin into positive spin.

- Create and sustain a generous state of mind.

- Keep new-love playfulness alive.

- Embrace differences as a way to express love and strengthen your bond.

- Honor and protect your relationship as something bigger than the two of you.

- Experience personal growth in ways that enrich and strengthen your bond.

- Deal with habits that might otherwise drive each other crazy.

- Cope with in-laws, children, friends, and other "fellow travelers."

You now know everything you need to know to keep score the right way.

In the next three chapters we'll be taking a look at how, in everyday life, you can score Frequent Foreplay Miles time and time again. And, don't forget to visit my blog and website at www.FrequentForeplayMiles.com for more tips on how you can consistently rack 'em up. Before moving on, however, take the time to do this chapter's exercise. It will help the Frequent Foreplay Miles philosophy really sink in and become second nature.

Exercise

Do this exercise whether you decide to track or not. It's good training for implementing Frequent Foreplay Miles into your relationship.

Here's what I want you to do:

Go back to Part A of the Chapter 1 exercise. For each entry you made, do step 3, i.e., prepare for a tracker discussion. Don't worry. I'm not going to ask you to actually have the discussion!

Here's an example:

Behavior: Repainted the front door after I had painted it.

Emotion: Hurt

Description: I voluntarily took on the job of painting the front door which we had agreed needed to be done. It was my project and when my sweetheart repainted it, it made me feel as though (s)he thought I hadn't done a good job and that I wasn't competent to do so.

Frequent Foreplay Miles Deduction: -55

Penalty: 5

Explanation of Penalty: My sweetheart has a habit of lending a "helping" hand where none has been requested and sometimes isn't wanted.

Here's how your analysis, in preparation of your discussion, might sound:

Another way to look at this is that my sweetheart wants to be helpful and for that I will change the deduction to an award. After all, the door did need a second coat of paint. If I ask myself whether there's any evidence on which to base my belief that my sweetie thinks I'm incompetent, I have to admit that (s)he doesn't say things that make me feel that way. Perhaps that belief comes from my sweetheart being too zealous in wanting to help me. It's great that (s)he wants to help and I don't want to quash that spirit so instead of penalizing my sweetheart, I'll say thanks with an award of Frequent Foreplay Miles. Then I'll explain to my sweetie that, according to my Foreplay Navigator, I like to finish the jobs I start so I can feel proud of my accomplishments and would prefer that (s)he ask before lending a hand. And, I'll be sure to give him/her an award of Frequent Foreplay Miles every times that happens.

*5

Frequent Foreplay Miles and Everyday Life: Communication

In the last analysis, what we are communicates far more eloquently than anything we say or do.

Steven R. Covey

Now that you know how to keep score the right way, you're excited about rackin' up Frequent Foreplay Miles. That's great. It's exactly what I hoped for. Now, let's take a look at some everyday issues and how Frequent Foreplay Miles can help you on your path to Total Intimacy. Those issues fall into three categories: Communication, Cohabitation, and (my favorite) Celebration. Here we go . . .

If it's one thing you do every day, it's communicate—or at least you try to. As George Bernard Shaw said, "The single biggest problem in communication is the illusion it has taken place." How many times have you or your sweetheart said, "That's not what I meant!"

Let me give you a great example. When Dale first began spending nights at my house, he used the guest bathroom. One morning, as I was heading for my shower, he asked, "Can we shower at the same time?" "Sure!" I responded enthusiastically and then quickly hopped into my shower and waited for him. Minutes later the water went ice cold and I learned just how effective "taking a cold shower" can be. What I *heard* was, "Can we shower together?" What he *meant* was, "Can we run both showers at the same time?" After the cold-water shock that brought me back to reality, I quickly figured out what happened and we were able to laugh about it.

Too often, however, couples cross wires and they don't realize it, or worse, the misunderstanding results in long-term resentment. Time and again I've seen wire-crossed couples engage in intimacy-trashing, circular, no-right-answer, unwinnable arguments over who said or promised what and who failed to deliver. Your Foreplay Back-Pocket Guide is designed to help you stay out of that trap. Let's take a look.

Promises, Expectations & Hope: These are Not the Same

When you utter the words "I will [fill in the blank]" you have made a promise to [fill in the blank]. Keeping the big promises to love, honor, cherish and be faithful are critical to the health and longevity of the relationship. Equally as important, however, are the everyday promises—"I'll be home by six," or "I'll pick up the dry cleaning," or "I'll never again throw my wet towel on the bed." Getting home at 6:30 when you promise to be home by 6:00 won't cause the earth to tilt on its axis, but to the sweetheart who has prepared a cheese soufflé that will fall if not served on time, that 30 minutes will ruin dinner, her evening, and your Frequent Foreplay Miles account. Forgetting to stop by the dry cleaners may rank low on your so-what scale, but not to the sweetheart who has the most important meeting of his life and wants to wear his "lucky" suit.

To LOCK in Frequent Foreplay Miles, keep your promises. Seems simple enough—until we zoom in. When a promise is expressly made, there's a bright line between keeping and breaking it. But that line gets fuzzy when the promise is implied through behavior or inferred from circumstances. For example, if Lisa borrows Bill's screwdriver from his shop, there's an implied promise that she will return it. Fair enough—but when? Bill may expect to see his screwdriver reappear within the next 10 minutes, but his expectation does not equal her promise. Lisa may think that returning the screwdriver when she's finished her project three hours later is good enough. In the meantime, Bill's been stewing for two hours and fifty minutes. When Kerri and Dan were having a backyard BBQ and he promised to help, she thought that meant hosing down the patio and peeling the potatoes for the salad. However, his idea of helping was to keep the kids out of her hair while she hosed down the patio and peeled the potatoes. This he-thought/ she-thought clash led to an argument that ended in tense detente only minutes before guests began to arrive. Neither of them was fully able to enjoy their own party.

Morphing your expectation or hope into a promise by assuming your sweetheart's Foreplay Navigator reads like yours will lead to countless misunderstandings. A great example of this came from my clients Camille and Mark. They had recently married, had children by prior marriages, and wanted to create an estate plan. Mark was the wealthier spouse, while Camille's estate was modest. Mark wanted to provide for Camille if he died first but also wanted his children to ultimately benefit from his estate. At our meeting I explained that on his death, his assets could be placed in a trust from which Camille would receive income and then, upon her later death, the remaining trust assets would be distributed to his kids. I found myself irritated with Camille because she couldn't—or chose not to—understand despite my extensive efforts to explain the trust.

Finally, I asked Mark to leave the room so I might have a private word with Camille. When I asked if there was something she needed to tell me, she said, "Mark promised to take care of me if he died." I told her I thought he was keeping that promise, but she replied, "He's not! My children are an essential part of me, and Mark's not leaving anything to my kids. Although the trust provides for me, it doesn't allow me to give so much as a dime to my children. I want to provide for them as much as Mark wants to provide for his kids." According to *her* Foreplay Navigator, Mark's promise to provide for Camille included her children—that's what she expected. But Mark's promise and his actions were based on *his* Foreplay Navigator, which differed on this important point. Once I understood what was holding Camille up, I called Mark back into my office and asked if he would be willing to pay the premiums on a life insurance policy for Camille so she could provide for her children. He was. Problem solved. They left my office arm-in-arm.

When it seems as though your partner is not keeping a promise you think was made, refer to your Foreplay Back-Pocket Guide and ask yourself how you can help your sweetheart ACE Frequent Foreplay Miles, and what you can DO so you both get Frequent Foreplay Miles. You'll be reminded to fall back on constructive candor. Had Camille simply spoken up, the planning process would have been easier and the frustration level would have been zero. Fortunately, I was there to interpret the situation. Without that help, Camille may have spent her entire married life thinking Mark had reneged on his promise to provide for her.

Your Foreplay Back-Pocket Guide is designed to keep you flying right. Consult it. That's exactly what my client Andrea did and because she did, she and Jay were $1.5 million richer. Here's what happened: Jay religiously played the lottery, always with the same numbers. One morning he asked Andrea to pick up a lottery ticket because it was the last day before the drawing, and he had to work late and wouldn't have time to pick up a ticket himself.

She promised to do so on her way home from work. That evening it was rainy and cold, her feet hurt, she was tired from a frustrating day, and she was in no mood to waste time on something she thought was pretty darned silly. Her plan was to "forget." As she drove past the market, a little voice said, "Andrea, you made a promise. If you break that promise, Jay will be upset and you're going to lose Frequent Foreplay Miles." With a heavy sigh, she made a U-turn, parked, and trudged through the rain on aching feet to buy the lottery ticket that won *$1.5 million.* Try to imagine how long it would have taken Andrea to recoup the 1.5 million Frequent Foreplay Miles she would have lost had Jay sat empty-handed, watching his winning numbers come up. Whew!

Use your Foreplay Back-Pocket Guide and don't forget that you and your sweetie have different Foreplay Navigators. Before you decide your partner is a low-down promise-breaker, be sure you're not morphing an unexpressed expectation or hope into a promise. And be careful, thoughtful, and clear in giving and keeping everyday promises—big and small. If you do, you'll build the trust that is the foundation for Total Intimacy.

The Pitfalls of The Question
(And Yes, Your Partner Really is Clueless)

It's worth knowing you're from different planets, and that men and women think differently because their brains are wired differently, but broad-brush generalizations and gender stereotypes only take you so far in decoding your one-and-only. For example, my ex never went to his cave. He'd talk it out until I threatened to hang myself, and only when I was tying the noose would he stop.

To know all the ways in which your sweetie breaks rather than fits the mold, you need his or her Foreplay Navigator. Unfortunately, no matter how much you know, you're bound to say or do something so far off the mark that you end up in an emotional no-fly zone. Without warning, your sweetheart is glaring at you, steam pouring out of his or her ears. You know you've screwed up, but you have no idea how. You innocently ask The Question—"What's the matter?"—and your sweetheart responds as if you just swallowed a big draft of "stupid" juice. Face it: if your sweetheart is so upset that (1) it's clear something is wrong, but (2) he or she hasn't told you why, then you've probably missed a page of your partner's Foreplay Navigator. You're definitely off course, and whether you've screwed up knowingly or unknowingly, you'll have to do some fancy flying to get back on track.

Here's an example: Myra and Luke agreed they would each have 50 wedding invitations to send to the guests of their choice. Myra's list included an ex-boyfriend with whom she had remained friendly. It wasn't until the wedding reception that Luke learned Myra had invited her former beau. That night, when they were finally alone, Luke went quiet, successfully cueing Myra to ask, "What's the matter?"

"What were you thinking when you invited that guy?" Luke exploded. According to his Foreplay Navigator, anyone with the IQ of a zucchini would know one does not invite a former sweetheart to one's wedding, no matter how friendly the relationship. According to Myra's Foreplay Navigator, however, inviting a former boyfriend-turned-friend was no big deal, and she was shocked to learn that Luke's opinion of her behavior was so low. This conflict of Foreplay Navigators did not warm the fires of their wedding night, and it took both effort and willpower on both their parts to get the relationship back on track.

When your sweetheart does something that makes you wonder if he or she has had a lobotomy, maybe it's because you're from different planets—but it's more likely a simple difference in Foreplay Navigators. Violations, resulting in mild irritation to thoughts of divorce (if not homicide), are inevitable but rarely intentional. They often happen because we are flying on autopilot, simply reacting to life's unpredictable circumstances. For example, Robert knows not to swear in front of Vicky's very conservative parents, but when he was once driving them all to a restaurant, he ran over a curb and "Oh, *&%^#$," popped out of his mouth before he realized it. (As they say, *&%^#$ happens!)

It's human nature (albeit not very mature) that when we're bent out of shape, we like to pout, sigh heavily, go silent, or in some nonverbal fashion cue the other that it's time to ask The Question. For instance, my mother has brought my father coffee in bed every morning for the 65 years they've been married. Well, almost every morning. The first time she failed to deliver, he waited a loooooooooong time before figuring out that her nose was out of joint about something. Undelivered coffee is how my mother cues my father to ask, "What's the matter?"

A better response than undelivered coffee, an ill-timed explosion, or the silent treatment is *constructive candor.* Here's a great example. Marie decided it was time to organize the closet. When she tossed some of Darren's clothing into the Goodwill bag, she thought she was doing a good thing for both charity and Darren. When she proudly mentioned what she had done, Darren's knee-jerk reaction was annoyance. He had no argument with what Marie had given away, but he felt that when it came to his things, it was his decision to make. He felt himself headed for a sulk. Luckily, he remembered to consult his Foreplay Back-Pocket Guide and instead said, "Marie, you are one of the most generous people I know and I think it's great that you support Goodwill. Next time, however, I'd like to be a part of the decision about what of mine is given away, okay?" "Sure," she said, happy that Darren supported her charitable efforts. Note the "constructive" in Darren's "candor." It would have been candid for Darren to say, "Marie, I don't appreciate your giving my things away and I think you were presumptuous," but it wouldn't have been constructive. Good job, Darren.

When you're on the receiving end of you've-done-me-wrong behavior, it's easy to roll your eyes, dismiss the behavior, or, worse, respond in kind. But remember this: your sweetheart is behaving that way because something you said or did, probably inadvertently, resulted in hurt, anger, disappointment, or all three. Regardless of your intention, it's better to resolve a clash of Foreplay Navigators than to allow a misunderstanding to morph into long-term resentment or a grudge that interferes with Total Intimacy. When you respond to your sweetie's *emotions* rather than the behavior, you amass Frequent Foreplay Miles instead of losing them. Consulting your Foreplay Back-Pocket Guide helps you do just that.

On the flip side, when your partner asks The Question, respond honestly and openly. Making your partner beg with evasive responses, such as, "Nothing!" is just down-right childish. Let your sweetheart in. Don't push him or her away by being snide, snarky, difficult, or argumenta-tive. Remember, it's the courageous sweetheart who sin-cerely asks The Question knowing that the answer means hearing how he or she has screwed up. Like Darren, reward that bravery with a straight-up, straightforward, construc-tively candid answer. For example, if the love of your life informs you his mom is coming to visit the same week that you have to get ready for the biggest work presentation of your life, when he sees your dismay and asks The Ques-tion, instead of storming out of the room and throwing a sarcastic remark over your shoulder—"Just what I need, to have to coddle your demanding mother when I'm up to my ears in work!" you might take a deep breath and say, "Honey, I truly appreciate that you want your mother and me to be closer—but I'm going to be tied up at the office almost every night that week. Next time, could you consult me before you invite her to stay with us?" Your lover may have to scramble to change mom's plans, but you've been honest with him both in terms of what you want (to be consulted) and what you need (to focus on your work during that week).

Think of these what-were-you-thinking-moments as gifts. They present opportunities to learn more about what makes each other tick. It's like an ache in a molar: the pain is nature's way of letting you know you need to have that tooth looked at for good dental health. When you feel the "pain," instead of lashing out, look at it as a chance for both partners to learn more about and share Foreplay Navigators. The more you do that, the fewer what-were-you-thinking-moments you'll have.

The Talk—and Avoiding the Argument

"We need to talk." These dreaded words seldom mean you need to talk about what movie to see or what to have for dinner. They mean your partner wants to have The Talk about how you've messed up or a particularly thorny issue your sweetie has been chewing on, such as whether it's time to have another child or whether to invite your mother-in-law to move in.

The Talk is emotionally charged because (1) it addresses a difficult issue, (2) it starts with someone feeling angry or hurt, or (3) it makes you uncomfortable. For these reasons, it's all too easy for The Talk to progress to The Argument. Arguing is not a bad thing per se, but if not done fairly it puts the kibosh on intimacy. There are many good resources on how to fight fairly (check out my website for several suggestions) so I'm not going to discuss fair fighting here, except for one critically important point. We've been taught that sticks and stones can break our bones, but words can never hurt us. That is unmitigated baloney. Words hurt, especially when coming from someone who is supposed to love you, to whom you are emotionally vulnerable, and in whom you have placed your trust.

Words can destroy intimacy just as quickly and effectively as infidelity. The smart sweetheart uses them, listens to them, and responds to them thoughtfully. Be careful to say what you mean and mean what you say or you'll never get the result you want. For example, Jim's way of dealing with disagreements was to dismiss Regina by saying, "If you don't like it, you can leave." After hearing that once too often, Regina met Jim at the door one evening when he arrived home from work. Her bags were packed and she said, "I'm about ready to leave. You can keep the kids, the house, and the dog. You also can take care of them, since you have all the answers." He got the message.

This is not rocket science. I don't have to tell you (or at least I hope I don't) that "You are being such a jerk!" is not conducive to a peaceful outcome even if it happens to be true. Having said that, you need to be on the lookout for situations when The Talk may be Act II, and in Act I something—maybe even a lot—has already gone wrong and emotions are raw. One of you has committed a what-were-you-thinking faux pas, or one or both of you has been privately stewing, or there are circumstances that make The Talk absolutely necessary if tricky.

Sometimes the sweetheart who needs to have The Talk can't muster the courage to get things started and instead will do something to set the stage. Truthfully, many of us prefer hard labor to talking about what bothers us. Therefore, we let our resentment simmer until, like the valve on a pressure cooker, we let off steam by picking a fight over a small, unrelated, typically unimportant issue. The ensuing anger gives us the false courage needed to have The Talk. Here's a great example: Garrett dreamed of starting his own business, but he and Kathryn (a stay-at-home mom) had one kid in college, one kid just a year away from college, and another about to start high school. He stoically put up with a job he hated and squelched his dream in favor of a steady paycheck. One morning Kathryn casually commented about all she had to do that day. Garrett uncharacteristically responded with a snide comment that, unlike him, she was free to do as she pleased, and, by the way, when in her busy schedule did she plan to find the time to clean the house because he was sick and tired of all the disorder! During the ensuing argument Kathryn realized that the real issue was not her housekeeping but Garrett's dissatisfaction with his work. She tamped down her you-are-being-such-a-jerk anger and allowed The Talk about Garrett's career path to begin. Once the real issue was on the table, The Talk successfully resulted in a plan of action for Kathryn to get a job and for Garrett to put in motion the steps necessary to start his own business.

There are two lessons to learn from this example:

1. It's important to determine what The Talk is really about and to ignore Act I as nothing more than your partner's nervous and frightened effort to get things going. The more often you avoid turning Act I into The Argument, the easier it will become for both of you to initiate The Talk in a healthier way.

2. It's not healthy to delay having The Talk. We goofball humans will avoid doing things that are good for us because they're not fun and maybe even painful. That's why there's ice cream in your freezer, your vegetable bin is empty, and you've got those extra pounds hanging around your waistline. I understand the reluctance to have The Talk when you know it will be emotionally charged and perhaps unpleasant. But consider this: if you have a cancerous tumor, surgery may be painful, but putting it off can kill you. Unresolved, cancerous issues have the same effect on your relationship.

If you find yourself preoccupied with worries, concerns, fears, resentment, anger, or other feelings that cause distance between you and your partner, it's time—maybe past time—for The Talk. Having The Talk can make you feel scared and vulnerable, but like medical treatment when you're sick, it is sometimes necessary to the health of your relationship.

When you've got a subject big enough for The Talk, consult your Foreplay Back-Pocket Guide before you open your mouth. Ask yourself how you can initiate and conduct The Talk so that you both earn Frequent Foreplay Miles. When you hear, "We need to talk," ask yourself what you can DO to LOCK in those Frequent Foreplay Miles. If you both come to The Talk with your Foreplay Back-Pocket Guide in hand, you'll find that you don't end up in The Argument. Instead, The Talk can create some of the most rewarding, enriching moments in your relationship. Tackling tough decisions, resolving thorny issues, and navigating troubled waters strengthens your relationship unlike nothing else. It's what makes you a team and reminds you that you are stronger for having committed yourselves to each other.

A Million Ways to Say, "I Love You"

Differences in Foreplay Navigators on how to say "I love you" can result in a downhill spiral to divorce. After years of working with couples, I've come to believe that a major— if not the major—source of relationship misunderstanding comes from Foreplay Navigators that differ on how to give and receive love. We all want affirmation that we are loved, and we want our gestures of love to be understood for what they are.

You would think that, "I love you," is simple enough to say and to understand. But, like all other communication, this seemingly simple message can get lost in translation. Bryan almost never said those three little words and when Katie did, he responded with, "Me too." She interpreted this as Bryan's lack of emotional commitment—until she consulted her Foreplay Back-Pocket Guide and was able to

NAVIGATE from negative to positive spin. Keeping Bryan's Foreplay Navigator in mind, Katie realized that Bryan's extreme shyness made it difficult for him to express tender emotions. "Me too" was his way of saying, "I love you." Instead of feeling disappointed that Bryan didn't speak her Foreplay Navigator language, she adopted his. "Me too" became their special way of saying, "I love you." Once, when Bryan was about to give a speech Katie winked at him and said, "Me too." It didn't matter that her words were out of context for those within earshot. To shy and nervous Bryan, it was exactly what he needed to help calm his nerves. He walked to the lectern and delivered a killer speech. Later that evening when they were alone, Katie said, "Bryan, I was really proud of you tonight." With tears in his eyes, he hugged her and whispered, "I love you." Wow.

Dale tells me he's proud of me as much or more often as he says he loves me. That lets me know two things. First, the obvious—he is proud of me. Equally as important, he's letting me know that, according to his Foreplay Navigator, expressing pride is a way of expressing love. I am proud of him, too. For the record, he's a fabulous cook, a great horn player, a wonderful husband, the best grandfather a kid could have, an entertaining storyteller, and the nicest person I have ever known. I am a lucky woman. Without his love, and his support, you wouldn't be reading this book right now and that's the truth.

Some partners don't *feel* the love because they don't *see* the love. Consider Stuart and Jenna. When she complained that he never told her he loved her, he was dumbfounded and said, "What are you talking about? I may not give you those mushy cards you're so fond of but I show my love every day by kissing you good-bye in the morning, running our errands on my lunch hour, helping when I get home, and doing the things I do for you and our kids." According to Stuart's Foreplay Navigator, being an involved and helpful partner was the ultimate expression of how much he cared. But according to Jenna's Foreplay Navigator, romantic and sentimental gestures were the language of love. Once they understood they had different "languages," Jenna saw Stuart's efforts to be involved and helpful as the gestures of love they were, and she remembered to show her appreciation. Stuart stopped by Hallmark, stocked up on mushy cards and remembered to say, "I love you," with romantic gestures more often.

Differences in Foreplay Navigators on how to say "I love you" can result in a downhill spiral to divorce. According to Drew's Foreplay Navigator, it is important to say it aloud. It was his habit to say, "I love you" at the end of every phone conversation, at the end of every day, and each time he walked out the door. Linda would respond in kind often enough to satisfy Drew's Foreplay Navigator, but according to her Foreplay Navigator, love is demonstrated non-verbally. She made Drew's favorite French toast on Sunday mornings, dropped off his dry cleaning, and picked up his dirty socks from the floor and put them in the hamper. Because Drew was not as attentive about the little things, Linda didn't feel the love. She began to dismiss Drew's proclamations of love as insincere and stopped responding in kind. As a result, Drew began to feel insecure. The more insecure and resentful he felt the more withdrawn he became, and the less he did for Linda. They found themselves arguing frequently. When one of them first mentioned the word "divorce," they realized how fragile their relationship had become.

You might think that their relationship wasn't very solid if all it took to get Linda and Drew back on track was learning how to say, "I love you." But if the foundation upon which a building is constructed begins to crack, the structural integrity of the whole building is compromised. Mutual love is the foundation upon which your relationship is built. If that foundation is cracked by doubt and resentment, the structural integrity of your relationship is at risk. Keeping your foundation strong by affirming your mutual love according to each other's Foreplay Navigator is critical to Total Intimacy.

Don't forget Question #2 of your Foreplay Back-Pocket Guide: "How can I help my sweetheart ACE Frequent Foreplay Miles?" Tell your sweetheart what makes you feel loved. At the very least, be sure to reinforce the positive when your sweetie hits a bull's eye by giving him or her a truckload of Frequent Foreplay Miles. Your partner wants to please you, and when you say, "Hey, I like that!" you're bound to get more of the same.

How can you LOCK in Frequent Foreplay Miles? Acknowledge your sweetheart's loving gestures, pay attention to how your sweetheart expresses love, and reciprocate in kind. Does she go to the rodeo with you even though she would never go otherwise? If so, show your appreciation by showing up with tickets to the ballet she enjoys. If he cooks your favorite dish, ask for a second helping and surprise him with the rum raisin ice cream he adores. If she rubs your back when you're tired, say thanks with a bear hug, and the next time she's running low on energy, make her favorite tea. When you acknowledge your partner's loving gestures, you'll get more of the same. When you consistently tell and show your sweetheart how much he or she is loved using your sweetheart's Foreplay Navigator as your guide, you'll get the message across in a big way. The Frequent Foreplay Miles you accumulate because of telling/showing how much you love your sweetheart in his or her style, not yours, are the most valuable Frequent Foreplay Miles you will ever accumulate.

Constructive Criticism Seldom Is

"You have more butt than you need, but you have a nice shape." That's the closest Dale has come to criticizing me and to be honest his comment was merely a verbal observation of fact. I now have more butt than when the comment was made, but he's never said another word about it. Bless him.

Coupling up bestows permission to say things (e.g., about your sweetie's butt) that might not otherwise be appropriate. However, there's a thin line between comments like Dale's and criticism. Criticism trashes emotional intimacy. Why? Because to be justified in criticizing another person, the following must be true:

- You are right and the other person is wrong,
- You are superior in position or knowledge, and
- You have the right to voice criticism and demand certain behavior.

Your sweetheart's boss, drill sergeant, mother, coach, personal trainer, or professor may meet that criteria but, as your partner's side-by-side equal, you do not. What you are (or should be) is the one person on the planet whom your partner can always, hands-down, absolutely, no questions asked, no doubt about it, count on for support. If you want emotional intimacy (and who doesn't) then never, ever cause your partner to question that support.

You know that shouting, "You're lazy!" is more likely to result in the cold shoulder than in the help around the house you're hoping to get. "No, honey, you're wrong," won't endear you to your partner. "You could lose a few pounds," is likely to get you cut off from you-know-what for several weeks! We all know that overt criticism plays havoc with intimacy. It's those situations where we're tempted to give "constructive criticism" that are tricky. Here's an example: Joshua was bummed when, in his annual review, the boss said Joshua was too independent. When he told April about it, she responded with, "Well, that sucks to hear. But, truthfully, sweetheart, playing well with others is not your strong point. I guess you need to work on that." April's observation may have been entirely accurate and the criticism meant constructively, but it was not well received. Joshua, in his funk, interpreted April's comment as siding with the boss, who at that moment was public enemy #1. And you can guess what that made her!

To be supportive, April didn't need to rant about how clueless the boss must be if he can't see that Joshua is his most valuable employee. Going to the flip-side extreme of criticism rings hollow and insincere. In such a situation, it's best to just listen and until asked for advice and help, keep your thoughts to yourself. If asked, the best response is one that is helpful and supportive WITHOUT a single critical word, e.g., "Maybe there's a book you can read about team playing in the corporate world." It's not up to you to point out or confirm your sweetheart's flaws, to tell him or her how to fix those flaws, or give your opinion on how your sweetheart can be a better person. It's up to you to provide the loving and supportive environment that allows your sweetheart to be the best that he or she can be according to his or her (not your) Foreplay Navigator.

Remember, you do not have a pipeline to The Truth and your opinions are not universal laws by which your sweetheart (or anyone else for that matter) is bound. "Constructive criticism" is just another term for "opinion." Your sweetheart may be endlessly fascinated by your opinion about everything from the state of the union to the entertainment value of demolition derby, but will lose interest when hearing your opinion about how he or she can improve. Your constructive criticism will cause your sweetie to emotionally withdraw, creating a barrier to Total Intimacy.

If you're running your first marathon and finish last, will you feel more supported and encouraged to do it again if your sweetheart says, "I'm so proud of you!" or says, "Nice effort, but your form could stand some improvement." Maybe your form sucked. Maybe your sweetheart is right. But which comment is more likely to put a smile on your face and make you feel like taking on the challenge again? Be a 24/7 cheerleader to your sweetheart and let the criticism—constructive or otherwise—come from somewhere else. When you're tempted to give criticism, constructive or otherwise, that's a great time to ask yourself Question #1—"How can I LOCK in Frequent Foreplay Miles?" In most cases, the answer will be to keep it zipped.

To be emotionally intimate, you must be connected. Criticism severs that connection and has no place in an intimate relationship. When it comes to your sweetheart, Noel Coward said it best: "I love criticism just so long as it's unqualified praise."

With Frequent Foreplay Miles you can communicate everything from profound love, to heart-bruising disappointment or seeing-red anger, to the everyday exchanges that really make or break a relationship. Telling your partner, "If you mention how wonderful your ex is one more time, I'm going to dock you 500 Frequent Foreplay Miles!" is a lot better than screaming, "If she's so great, why aren't you still married to her?!?!!" And it's fun to shape your darling's behavior with the carrot of Frequent Foreplay Miles—"Let me go out with the boys on Saturday and you'll earn a thousand FFMs and dinner with your mother."

What's more, when it comes to everyday communication, you and your partner say and do things all day long that are heard and interpreted by the other—mostly accurately, sometimes not. The miscues are often unimportant, produce no damage, and, like my cold shower, sometimes result in a good laugh. But when that's not the case and you feel the first twinge of a negative emotion, you need to immediately consult your Foreplay Back-Pocket Guide. Can you NAVIGATE in a positive direction? If not, then what can you DO to LOCK in Frequent Foreplay Miles, help your sweetie ACE Frequent Foreplay Miles, and make sure you both win?

Keep your Foreplay Back-Pocket Guide handy. The more you know and honor differences with your Guides in hand, the richer your relationship will be.

*6

Frequent Foreplay Miles and Everyday Life: Cohabitation

All marriages are happy. It's trying to live together afterward that causes all of the problems.

Shelley Winters

Sharing a bed is a wonderful thing. Sharing all other spaces presents count-to-ten challenges. Katherine Hepburn said, "I often wonder whether men and women really suit each other. Perhaps they should live next door and just visit now and then." She may have a point, and that would certainly resolve the how-to-decorate and how-to-maintain issues but, fact is, most of us prefer one nest. You've learned that for the clever, paying-attention sweetheart, differences and challenges are opportunities to pick up Frequent Foreplay Miles. Sharing space proves the point.

His, Hers and Ours

There's a reason why the towels say "His" and "Hers." No matter how physically intimate you are and what body fluids you may be exchanging, there are some things you don't want to share. Dale doesn't mind sharing toothbrushes but he doesn't like it when I use his towel. I find that weird. You use a toothbrush because your teeth need cleaning but you use a towel *after* you're clean. I don't mind if Dale uses my towel on his clean body but it grosses me out if he uses my toothbrush on his dirty teeth. We all have our little quirks. Don't try to figure out the why and the what-for of quirks, just LOCK in Frequent Foreplay Miles by respecting them.

There's a "His" and "Hers" stamped on more than towels, albeit invisibly. Remember that the next time you're tempted to read her journal when she's at the grocery store or peek at his email when he's mowing the lawn. Journals and email may be left in plain view and your sweetheart probably isn't hiding a thing, but unless you've been given express permission to take a look, such things are private and you need to keep your hands and eyes off. Ditto for snail mail, purses, briefcases, boxes of mementos, and so on.

"His" and "Hers" are usually clearly defined. "Ours" gets complicated, beginning with combining households. What makes this tricky is that it isn't like negotiating whether to go to Spain or France on your vacation. It's easy enough to compromise by spending time in each place. However, it's much more difficult to split the difference when you're negotiating where to live, what to keep, and what to toss out. Unless you're right out of the college dorm or your parents' home, you've both got a houseful of furniture, art, knickknacks, and 'fess up, a ton of crap. The molded-to-your-backside recliner with cup holder and duct-tape-repaired rip…the tattered-but-beloved bed canopy your great-grandmother crocheted in the previous century…the paint-by-number landscape your grown-up son did as a ten-year old…the ceramic frog collection you started as a kid that now occupies an entire bookcase…it's crap, but it's your crap and you're attached to it. It's no small task to find a place for all that stuff from two households, much less resolve conflicting tastes and mix early American milk glass with contemporary chrome in a way that works for both of you.

Since you can't cut the La-Z-Boy in two, toss half, and park the other in the living room, you have a choice. You can see the process of combining stuff as a series of negotiations in which someone wins and someone loses, or you can see it as a win-win situation where one of you gets to keep the whatever and the other scores Frequent Foreplay Miles. If you approach negotiations from this perspective, you'll find yourselves each giving in a little, and before you know it, you'll have your cozy nest just the way it should be, recliner, ceramic frogs and all.

Combining households is just the beginning. Now you get to share the sofa, the TV screen (and the remote), the computer, the garage, the shower stall, the backyard, the refrigerator, the coffee pot, the toilet seat, the screwdriver, the toothpaste, the closet, and just about everything else in the house except your clothes (and even then, you may find that your sweetheart has "borrowed" your favorite sweatshirt). This can produce some interesting moments. For example, Laura subscribes to the axiom that there is a place for everything and everything in its place. But for Laura, it's not enough that everything is in its place. She wants the place, even if it's behind closed doors 99% of the time, to be neat, too. Her drawers and closets are beautifully organized. Need a safety pin? Laura not only knows where they are but the sizes are separated into little plastic boxes. When things are orderly, Laura feels peaceful. Disarray leaves her feeling unsettled and cranky. She reports that her husband Bert also believes that there's a place for everything, but with one twist: to Bert's way of thinking, the place for everything is wherever he happens to leave it.

Laura and Bert have had to resolve this fundamental difference in how their shared space should be maintained. They struck a compromise. What they refer to as the "common area," i.e., the area that would be seen by visitors, is maintained according to Laura's standards. The garage and Bert's office are his space and they can be maintained to his far less exacting standards. The "private space," i.e., the areas where guests are not likely to wander, are kept to a more relaxed standard. Laura's drawers and portion of the closet are as she wants them, and she turns a blind eye to Bert's drawers and his share of the

closet. They admit that neither one of them is perfect—
Laura occasionally gives in to the urge to straighten Bert's
sock drawer, and he sometimes leaves his shoes in the living room—but it works well enough.

How you share space can be a metaphor for the entire
relationship. If your sweetheart finds it distasteful to discover
nail clippings in the sink yet you routinely clip and leave,
you're probably inconsiderate in other ways, too. If you are
so rigid in your neatness standard that a coffee cup left on
the bathroom counter sends you into a tizzy, there's a darned
good chance you're uncompromising in other ways as well.
Take a few minutes to think about that. Do you need to
be more diligent in referring to your Foreplay Back-Pocket
Guide and pay more attention to your sweetheart's Foreplay
Navigator? A great place to start is right there at home. If it
makes her crazy when you leave your gym socks on the bathroom floor, pick 'em up and LOCK in Frequent Foreplay
Miles. If you find yourselves arguing about how you share
space, help your sweetheart ACE Frequent Foreplay Miles
by reinforcing the positive, and, whenever possible, always
NAVIGATE from the negative to the positive. Never forget
that the little stuff counts big time.

When Less is More

Hubby Dale and a guy friend sat on their boat knocking
down a few beers and whiled away a lazy afternoon by list-
ing body "ations"—urination, expectoration, perspiration,
etc. I tried, but failed, to imagine doing the same with a
girlfriend. We would identify the three most important

"ations"—exfoliation, ovulation and menstruation, three these two geniuses missed—and then go shoe shopping.

Like it or not, "ations" are part of life. When you're cheek by jowl it's impossible to pretend, as you do in those early getting-to-know-each-other days, that you're the only person on the planet who doesn't experience them. At some point, one or the other of you will fart, belch, or leave the bathroom in need of fumigation. One bit of relaxed behavior leads to another and before you know it, you're sharing—perhaps over-sharing—all those "ations" with your long-suffering sweetheart.

Dale never farted in front of me until just about a year after we started dating. When I mentioned this to him, he said it was because he had become comfortable around me, which I had always dismissed as bogus. But when I Googled "farting in front of your boyfriend/girlfriend," I found pages of articles and blog entries, many suggesting that farting in your sweetheart's presence is, indeed, a sign that you are comfortable in the relationship. Wow. Who would have thought?

As research for this book, I held a series of focus group discussions in which the subject of body functions was discussed. The topic always inspired much laughter, a little disgust, and great stories. For instance, Carla described being with a group of girlfriends who were complaining about their guys' flatulence. She was the only one whose honey had never once farted in her presence. She began to wonder if Herb was truly committed to the relationship, and she decided to ask him why he was so proper around her. His response was to raise a cheek and let one fly. They were married six months later. Herb has been happily farting ever since, and Carla was reminded that one should be careful what one asks for.

Humans, at an early age, develop a fascination with body functions. There's not a five-year old on the planet who doesn't giggle after farting. I know it's not fair to stereotype and I'll probably get in trouble for this, but in my experience guys never quite get over that middle-school fascination with body functions. There's even a certain pride that some men take in those "ations." For instance, my sister Jenny, who had fallen asleep on the couch, woke in the middle of the night and headed for bed. As she approached the bedroom door, Bill let a triple-flutter-blaster fly. She turned around and spent the rest of the night on the couch. When morning arrived and Jenny related this to Bill, he raised his fist in celebration of such a heroic fart. Dale still speaks in referential tones about the high school classmate who could fart while at the same time belching the tune to Wooly Bully. Dale also brags about the time he farted, coughed, belched and sneezed all at the same time. Happily, Dale has not attempted a repeat performance. While I have become a more tolerant spouse over the years, an "ation" of that scale would most assuredly trash Dale's Frequent Foreplay Miles account.

However, I admit it: body functions can be funny. Dale and I were at a Wednesday afternoon movie, the favorite showing for folks from the retirement community. During a quiet moment Dale coughed so hard he ripped one. A really loud one. The elderly woman in front of Dale reached up and patted her head as if she feared the blast had dislodged her wig. We could not stop laughing and had to leave.

Then there's grooming. In a perfect world, we'd all wake up as they do in the soaps—perfect hair, perfect make-up, no morning breath. You wouldn't need to floss or brush your teeth, clip your toenails, exfoliate, mud pack, shave, or file your calluses. However, as anyone can tell as they look over at their sweetie's bed head and sleep-encrusted eyes, or watches as the love of their life scratches his butt as he heads to the bathroom, it's soooooooooo not a perfect world.

Oddly, the one thing that grosses Dale out is watching me put my contacts on. You may consider that as weird as I do, but it does demonstrate an important point: when it comes to body functions and grooming, it's a good idea to know when you're crossing your sweetie's "that's disgusting" line. We all have one. Kathy is grossed out by teeth flossing, Elijah by ear wax on Q-Tips. Shirley needs complete privacy to groom her feet. Nail clippings make Rebecca want to hurl. To keep your Frequent Foreplay Miles balance healthy, respect your sweetheart's quirks and avoid the gross out.

It may be impossible to maintain the same level of propriety you would around a stranger, but remember this: in an intimate relationship, there are times when less is more. Rack up those Frequent Foreplay Miles by memorizing the page in your sweetie's Foreplay Navigator on body functions and grooming.

When Moods Collide

In even the best relationship there are times when your moods are out of sync. You're feeling randy, he's not. You think it's funny, she doesn't. Colliding moods often pass quickly with no residual damage. But there are times when the mood is more than momentary. You're feeling blue, restless, cranky, irritable, prickly, or out of sorts. If you were unattached, you could give in to your mood and watch TV wearing nothing but underwear, eat peanut butter straight from the jar, ignore the phone, watch ten nonstop hours of *The Three Stooges* or *I Love Lucy*, take a 3-hour bubble bath, play Guitar Hero for hours, pull every last stitch out of the closet in an I-have-nothing-to-wear-pity-party, or do whatever other self-indulgent thing you do when you're feeling sorry for yourself. Since you're not unattached, however, your sweetheart is in the fallout zone of your bad mood. Bad moods can lead to stupid arguments. Stupid arguments lead to lost Frequent Foreplay Miles. And lost Frequent Foreplay Miles lead to lost intimacy. Handling bad moods with finesse, however, can keep those Frequent Foreplay Miles rolling in.

Some moods are predictable. For example, Christine is a night owl, sleeps late, and wakes up slowly. Ernie springs out of bed as if he knows he will win the lottery that very day. Ernie's first-thing-in-the-morning cheerfulness is only slightly less irritating to Christine than a mosquito infestation. He finds her first-thing-in-the-morning crankiness childish and indulgent. This disconnect resulted in early morning arguments. They needed a solution. Now, she wears sunglasses in the morning and he doesn't speak to her until they come off. When they do, it's the signal that she's ready to be cheerful.

No discussion of predictable moods would be complete without mention of the monthly cycle to which women are subjected and which makes us feel everything from melancholy to homicidal. Well, guess what? Research suggests that men go through a monthly cycle, too. The lucky dogs may not have temporary water weight gain, but a regular drop in testosterone makes them lethargic and depressed. For both men and women, the best strategy for monthly cycles may be a healthy dose of tolerance combined with the mantra, "This, too, shall pass."

The savvy sweetheart simply lets the monthly mood run its course. More challenging is the unpredictable mood that is triggered by a bad day at the office, a hot day with high humidity (that one always does it for me), irritation with yourself for having been lazy about going to the gym (another favorite of mine), a dead car battery, a letter from the IRS, an unexpectedly scheduled meeting with your boss or a representative from human resources, the driver who cut you off, cat barf on the carpet, your teen's mouthy attitude, or just because.

When your honey becomes Mr. or Ms. Hyde, it's the perfect time to apply everything you know about your sweetheart's Foreplay Navigator. Whip out your Foreplay Back-Pocket Guide and ask yourself how you can LOCK in Frequent Foreplay Miles. Here are some examples:

- Dylan likes to be left alone so Tammy goes silent and, when possible, slips quietly into another room until Dylan goes to his happy place.
- Jeff paces, waves his arms, and rants, preferably to an audience. Deborah is the audience and says such things as, "That guy was a real jerk!" Deborah knows Jeff is back to the world of the reasonable when he responds to her verbal support by disagreeing with her, e.g., "He's not really a jerk. He was probably just having a bad day."
- Shelby busies herself with putting things in order by straightening the piles of paper on her desk, alphabetizing the spice cabinet, or matching loose socks in the drawer. Jamie wordlessly joins in the effort by sweeping the garage floor or organizing his tool bench.

It's one thing to take advantage of an understanding sweetheart's indulgence. It's quite another to push it too far. You need to know when to quit your bitchin', suck it up and behave yourself, or you run the risk of taxing your partner's patience and your own Frequent Foreplay Miles account.

There's a certain look Dale gives me when it's time for me to stop. He never says a word, just looks at me in a way that says, "Come on, by now you must realize just how childish and boorish you're being." It works.

Scott lets his wife Susie know he's had enough by saying, "I'm going in the other room now and I'm going to count to 10. Twice. Then I'll be back." If she's not ready to give up the funk, she goes to the bedroom until she's over it. If she is ready to give it up when Scott returns, they both go on with their day as if the mood never happened.

When you have Total Intimacy, you feel safe in being who you are at the moment—warts and all. You know that you are loved and it's okay to be less than perfect. But you keep your Frequent Foreplay Miles account solid when you don't take it for granted by pushing the boundaries.

In truth, your sweetheart's bad mood is a great opportunity to enhance intimacy. One of the critical elements of Total Intimacy is that you are each other's 24/7 cheerleaders—nurturing, loving, and supportive. In the context of bad moods, this means you don't treat the mood with indifference, disdain, amusement, or in any other way that belittles your sweetheart or diminishes the emotions underlying the mood. Even if your sweetheart is by any reasonable standard overreacting, foolish, silly, irrational, childish or otherwise inappropriate, it's not up to you to point this out. If given the space and freedom to just be in the mood, it's likely that your sweetheart will sooner rather than later realize that he or she is overreacting, foolish, silly, etc. By letting your sweetheart work it out, you'll earn Frequent Foreplay Miles by the zillions.

Like it or not, you fell in love with an imperfect human being who is not always charming, happy, or at the top of the good mood game. Learning how your sweetheart works through moods by discovering his or her Foreplay Navigator on this point will result in your getting—instead of losing—Frequent Foreplay Miles.

The Meltdown: Another Ticket to Relationship Intimacy

Just as a bad mood can strike without warning, things can unexpectedly go very wrong, providing justifiable cause for a good-mood-tailspin right into a full-fledged meltdown. The oven malfunctions, the appetizer burns, and your snooty in-laws will arrive any moment to a smoke-filled house. The TV with the gi-normous screen you've been bragging about goes on the fritz moments before kickoff and 22 of your buddies are about to miss the game of the century. You're leaving for your brother's wedding and the baby throws up on the perfect silk dress you shopped for months to find. The flight home from the conference your boss made you attend is late and you miss your own birthday party.

At such moments, we're sure there's a cosmic conspiracy to ruin our life and, thus, a meltdown is justified. To those not targeted by the conspiracy, however, a meltdown is likely to be seen as, well, the childish behavior that it is—but try telling that to an upset sweetheart and you're likely to have your head handed to you. It's just human nature. When things go wrong, people get upset.

Meltdowns are the response to disappointment. You hoped to be the perfect hostess to your in-laws, have the best football party ever, look beautiful at your brother's wedding, or make it home for your birthday party. A go-wrong got in the way and instead of fulfilled hope, you were disappointed. Sometimes the disappointment is the result of nothing you did and other times it's the result of disappointment in yourself. Here's an example: Norman's pride was the vintage Thunderbird he had lovingly restored. He was not keen on letting anyone drive it but he gave in to Joanne's pleas when she wanted to celebrate her best friend's engagement by taking her to lunch in the spiffy car. When they arrived at the restaurant and parked, Joanne was paying more attention to chatting excitedly about her friend's engagement than to the car and inadvertently left it in neutral. As the two friends walked toward the door, they heard loud shouting. Joanne turned and watched in horror as the car rolled down the slight incline of the street—and through the plate glass window of an antique store. She silently reached for her cell phone and, with more dread than she could have imagined, made the necessary call to Norman.

As you might imagine, Norman was some kind of ticked off. Fortunately, he had time to consult his Foreplay Back-Pocket Guide and ask himself how he could LOCK in Frequent Foreplay Miles. He knew Joanne would have berated herself for being careless. She would be feeling stupid and heartbroken that the T-Bird Norman had lovingly restored was damaged because of her negligence. His anger gave way to compassion and he wisely responded to how Joanne would be feeling rather than what she had done. When he arrived, he wrapped his arms around Joanne and said, "It's just a car and can be fixed. Are you okay?" Good call. The car has long ago been fixed, the insurance claim paid, and now Joanne and Norman have a great story about the irony of his vintage car ending up in an antique shop window. And talk about racking up Frequent Foreplay Miles! Norman scored big that day and, as Joanne shyly admitted, he scored that night, too.

When things go wrong and your sweetheart is disappointed, the key to racking up Frequent Foreplay Miles is responding to the underlying emotion rather than the behavior.

It gets a bit more dicey when what goes wrong happens to both of you. In that instance, the meltdown is up for grabs and goes to the first taker. Here's an example: Dale and I were traveling by rent-a-wreck from Point Nowhere to Point End-of-the-Earth in Patagonia. Midway, the car died. Just as I opened my mouth to lament that we would be robbed and left to die where our bodies would never be found, Dale had a 10-on-the-Richter-scale tantrum. He pounded the steering wheel, turned the air blue, blue, blue with his swearing, then got out of the car and began maniacally kicking it. I had been too slow on the uptake, he had called dibs on the meltdown, and therefore it was my turn to stay calm. I didn't try talking him off the ledge. I didn't point out that his behavior wasn't solving our dilemma. I let him enjoy the moment, supporting him by throwing in a few expletives of my own. He called losing-it-dibs. Fair is fair. Although I didn't get to have my meltdown, I've gotten good laughs from telling the story of when mild-mannered Dale went postal. When I tell it, I get to throw in my highway robbery fears. It worked out. It usually does.

Here's the rule: when what goes wrong happens to both of you, only one of you gets to have the meltdown. The other one stays calm. After all, someone has to deal with whatever it is that went wrong. Trust me on this. Following this rule is the best way to avoid an argument and the quickest way to get your crazed sweetie back to the world of the sane. In addition, knowing the signs of an incipient meltdown in your sweetie can help you beat him or her to the punch. For instance, Jean knows that Richard's meltdowns are preceded by a vein throbbing in his forehead. When one of the kids spilled cherry Kool-Aid all over the family room sofa and Richard's vein began to throb, she seized the opportunity to get the new sofa she'd been wanting and beat him to the fit-throwing punch. She figured Richard would more readily agree to a new sofa if she had the tantrum. She was right. Smart woman.

Remember, however, when things go wrong and you respond with a meltdown, the last thing you want to be told is that your behavior is ridiculous. So, the next time your love bug has a meltdown, return the favor. Giving your partner the space to be less than perfect without you being holier-than-thou judgmental is a great way to sustain intimacy. It says, "I love you, imperfections and all." And which of us doesn't love to hear that?

Humor: It Really Is the Best Medicine

If I wasn't a believer in the power of laughter before I met Dale, I am now. My guy regularly cracks me up. Even better, he thinks I'm funny, too. We are quick with one-line zingers and have matching funny bones—most of the time.

Here's an example: it was 1998, and we were one of five

couples on a five-night camping tour of the Manu Reserve, a rain forest in the Amazon basin. Dale was in heaven, but even though I thought it was cool to wake to the sound of howler monkeys and see poison dart frogs and army ants in their natural environment, I was miserable. I became even more miserable as it rained every day, almost continuously. As we motored up river, Lucinda and Graham— Londoners who had thought to bring a huge umbrella—were dry while the rest of us found little protection from the cheap, plastic ponchos we had bought in Cuzco. Lucinda and Graham were irrepressibly chipper. Of course they were. They were dry!

By the fifth morning, I was damp, cranky and, frankly, tired of Lucinda and Graham. When Dale attempted to joke with our non-English speaking guide, I grabbed him by the lapels, pulled his face close to mine, and said through clenched teeth, "You are not funny in the rain forest!" He didn't hesitate for a moment. He looked down at me and said, with a perfectly straight face, "Graham thinks I'm funny." I cracked up and my mood instantly improved.

Humor can get you through rough spots—even labor. When Georgia was enormously pregnant with her daughter, she was waddling toward her apartment while carrying two large bags of groceries. A guy walking toward her said, "Got a match?" Georgia was so intent on getting the groceries in the house that she didn't realize he was making a joke. Instead she said, "In my apartment," thinking it was darned inconsiderate of him to ask for a match when she obviously had her hands full. This nice guy followed Georgia so she could give him some matches, thanked her, and left—which is exactly when she realized how dumb she had been. When Georgia was in labor and in the midst of a particularly awful contraction her husband said, "Got a match?" She laughed, easing her discomfort.

Was there a time in your relationship when you were angry or irritated and took it out on your partner? Don't you wish you'd found the humor instead? Well, maybe it's not too late. Laughter is not only good for you in the here-and-now but it can heal past hurts, too. Let me give you an example. Dana and Jerry were married poolside in their backyard. Jerry had Jax, his beloved golden retriever, at his side. It was windy that day and during the ceremony one of Jax' favorite toys was blown into the pool. Jax did what retrievers do: he jumped into the pool, retrieved his toy, climbed out of the pool, dropped it at Jerry's feet—and then shook himself dry. Dana's beautiful wedding gown, Jerry's tux, and the minister were splattered with pool water. Dana was livid. When the guests left, she tore into Jerry about how his stupid dog had ruined her wedding day.

Fast forward to the four-month anniversary of their wedding. Dana regretted her post-wedding tirade and wanted to undo as much of the damage as possible. She served a lovely dinner poolside, and when she and Jerry were seated, Dana pulled a rubber bone from where she had it hidden, threw it into the pool and instructed Jax to fetch. He did, and in no time at all Dana, Jerry and the table were splattered with pool water. With water dripping down her face, Dana said to Jerry, "I'm sorry about my temper tantrum at our wedding. How about a mulligan?"

Jerry began to laugh and, forgetting all about dinner, they raced each other to the bedroom.

With a little creativity and a good sense of humor, Dana was sort of, kind of, able to turn back the clock and relive the situation. That's not always possible. So while I admit it's not always easy, I remind you that, in times of conflict and high stress, humor can save the day. Finding humor in a flat tire, a soaked wedding dress, a missed plane, the cat's coughed-up fur ball on the bed, a scheduling mishap, a flooded bathroom, screwed-up directions, an over-cooked appetizer, or the myriad other "spilled milk" situations you'll face as a couple can bring you closer together. Having said that, there's a fine line between laughing with and laughing at. Cross that line and your Frequent Foreplay Miles accounts will take a beating. If your sweetie slips and lands in a puddle on the way to the boss's house for dinner, laughing at his or her discomfort no matter how funny it looks will usually guarantee a frosty dinner and a night on the couch for you. On the other hand, helping your beloved see the funny side of the cat's fur ball or pen that exploded in a pocket can lighten the situation and add Frequent Foreplay Miles to your account. Once Felix was helping his wife Sam load the dishwasher after dinner. She turned too quickly to put something into a cabinet and ran her leg into the edge of the open dishwasher door. She grabbed her leg and let fly a few choice words. Felix immediately turned, pointed to the dishwasher and said, "Bad dishwasher! Bad, bad, bad!" Sam looked up, startled—and began to laugh. They finished the dinner dishes and repaired to the bedroom to "check her leg" (and the rest of her too).

Remember, humor, like beauty, is in the eye of the beholder. What we find funny, odd, weird, goofy, or whacky is different for each of us. We all have preferences. We also have little quirks, pet peeves, irksome annoyances, or what I lump under the category "peccadilloes," that others, including our sweetheart, may find humorous, silly, or downright ridiculous, but about which we are quite serious. Here are some examples of what I mean by peccadilloes:

- Norma goes crazy if the customer ahead of her in the supermarket checkout line fails to use the rubber bar to keep their order separate.

- Derek resents having to give his name when he places an order at Noah's Bagels or Starbucks and always gives a fake name.

- Bob eats his popcorn one kernel at a time.

- Kerry has made a map of her favorite grocery store and makes her shopping list in the order in which things appear in the store.

- Kevin puts the stamp upside down on envelopes he uses to pay bills.

- Melinda can't brush her teeth if anyone is watching.

Now, Kerry's husband thinks it's beyond weird that she's made a map of the grocery store—but it makes perfect sense to the ever-efficient Kerry. Melinda's boyfriend thinks it's odd that she doesn't mind peeing in front of him but he has to leave the bathroom when she brushes her teeth. The moral of the story? It's not likely that you're ever going to change your partner's mind about these things. So, right now, ask yourself Question #1—"How can I LOCK in Frequent Foreplay Miles?" There's only one good answer: Surrender. Laughter and shared humor bring you closer. Anger and irritation drive you apart. So lighten up. Have fun. Use your Foreplay Back-Pocket Guide to help you know when it's okay to laugh and when to quietly respect your partner's peccadilloes.

Going from "His" and "Hers" to "Ours" is a big decision. Melding your stuff and your lives presents challenges, no doubt about it. Finding your living-together groove by paying close attention to each other's Foreplay Navigator makes it a smoother, even rewarding, experience. Sure, there will be moments when you're nostalgic for the good-old-alone days so you could indulge in a bad mood, watch *The Three Stooges* instead of *Sleepless in Seattle*, leave the house a mess, or ignore your sweetheart's wishes, likes, dislikes, peccadilloes, moods, etc. That's to be expected. When, however, you consistently refer to your Foreplay Back-Pocket Guide, those moments will be far and few between. More often, your heart will swell with joy when you hear, "Hi, honey, I'm home."

*7

Frequent Foreplay Miles and Everyday Life: Celebration

The more you praise and celebrate your life, the more there is in life to celebrate.

Oprah Winfree

We often hear that being in a committed relationship is hard work. Baloney. True, we can make it hard work by focusing on the wrong things, such as trying to remodel our partner or being right. Instead, Totally Intimate couples don't spin their wheels on such futile endeavors. Totally Intimate couples celebrate their love, not just on their anniversary, but every day.

A recent study found that the older you are the happier you are. I'm not surprised. I've reached the big six-oh and I'm happier than I've ever been. I dress around my bunions and I do not care if my shoes are slightly less (okay, a lot less) fashionable than strappy little 5-inch stilettos. I'm a grandparent and happy about it. But here's the really cool thing: I may be creeping up on old age faster than I'd like, but I'm doing it with my best friend, my sweetheart, my lover, my hang out buddy. He's the guy who makes me laugh, who gets my jokes, who sighs with sympathy when my lower back aches, who doesn't care that I don't wear stilettos, and with whom I can while away hours on end with memories of the great times we've had and then plan more of the same. He's the guy who, as we're watching TV or at the movies, reaches out to hold my hand and with that quiet gesture says, "I love you." There's only one thing as good as those falling-in-love feelings, and that's the contented intimacy that comes with time and shared life.

The reward for hanging in there is the happiness and contentment that comes with having grown old together. Now that's something to celebrate!

Red Letter Days

In today's world of technology, there is no excuse for forgetting an important date. If you can't manage your own calendar, then sign up for an on-line service (such as bigdates. com) that will remind you of anniversaries, birthdays, and other special days, in plenty of time to acknowledge them in a way that jibes with your sweetheart's Foreplay Navigator.

When it comes to Red Letter Days, the trick to amassing Frequent Foreplay Miles is (1) knowing your sweetheart's special days, and (2) knowing how your sweetheart's Foreplay Navigator reads when it comes to celebrating them. I suggest you exchange a list of Red Letter Days. You may be surprised: one couple I know met on a Thursday, so he considers every Thursday a Red Letter Day. She initially thought it was a bit much to celebrate every Thursday but she indulged him. In one way or another, they acknowledge every Thursday as the day on which they first met. Maybe they have a candlelit dinner, maybe they shower together in the morning, maybe they just take time for an extra-long I-love-you hug, but every Thursday they celebrate how happy they are to be together. She no longer thinks every Thursday is a bit much. Wow!

Celebrating Red Letter Days with a Foreplay Navigator bull's eye is easy if you ask your sweetie how he or she feels about the subject. I have a friend who says, "Diamonds or divorce!" but I think she's kidding—at least a little bit. Seriously, when my clients Patrice and Leonard were first married, she told him she liked things that sparkled. Years later she had to tell Leonard to stop buying her jewelry, she had too much already. Imagine that! If you're unclear as to your partner's favorite way to celebrate, pay attention to how your love bug acknowledges your Red Letter Days. If on Valentine's Day she gives mushy cards, you'll score Frequent Foreplay Miles if you reciprocate with a romantic gesture. If he acknowledges your birthday with a surprise spa weekend, he probably values experiences. On his birthday, forget about a new drill and plan an experience he'll enjoy.

If your Foreplay Navigators are carbon copies of each other, you're lucky enough that you should consider playing the lottery. More often than not, however, one of you will be more sentimental, fonder of romantic gestures, more into gifts, etc. If you and your partner have very different Foreplay Navigators, a game plan is definitely in order. For example, Shannon is practical and watches every penny. While she enjoys celebrating Red Letter Days, she finds flowers a colossal waste of money and is one woman for whom the gift of a new toaster scores big. Her hubby Grady, on the other hand, is a softhearted romantic who loves to bring her flowers—*huge* bouquets of flowers. Because Shannon knows that Grady enjoys the romance of flowers, she suggested that instead of buying cut flowers, he buy a plant for the garden that (hopefully) won't die. Grady, being the romantic that he is, took the hint and began buying flowers in creative ways, e.g., a sexy nightie that has a flower pattern in the fabric or rose scented soap— things that the practical Shannon can use. And Shannon, who finds it difficult to spend money on frivolities, instead finds ways to be romantic that also serve a practical function, e.g., baking Grady's favorite cookies but in the shape of a heart or giving him silk sheets.

Earlier you learned that the best way to express love is the way your sweetheart is most likely to get the message. Ditto for celebrating Red Letter Days. If your style is vastly different from that of your sweetheart, then take the lead from Shannon and Grady. What's most important is that Red Letter Days are used to celebrate your life together. It doesn't matter how you do it, as long as you're both satisfied in the end.

It's also possible that one of you celebrates a particular Red Letter Day with more enthusiasm than the other. For instance, my friend Michelle loves Halloween. Every day for the entire month of October she wears a different Halloween sweater, her house is decorated to the max, and she looks forward to trick-or-treaters. As far as her husband is concerned, Halloween could be omitted from the calendar and not be missed. But instead of rolling his eyes when October 1st comes and Michelle drags out the decorations, he racks up Frequent Foreplay Miles by helping her. He then invites all their friends over so they can appreciate the decorations she works so hard to set up.

Red Letter Days can come on a regular schedule, or a Red Letter Day might be a once-in-a-lifetime or a once-in-awhile event. It's a Red Letter Day when…

- Her water color is accepted into the art exhibit.

- His team goes to the Super Bowl.

- She gets her PhD.

- He gets a promotion.

- You pay off the mortgage.

- His business is nominated for an excellence award.

- She makes her first sale.

- He runs his first 10K.

Celebrate those days, and remember, how you do it is far less important than just doing it. You undoubtedly will celebrate one Red Letter Day very differently from another. Your tenth wedding anniversary may call for a blowout blast with friends while the anniversary of your first date may call for a quiet, candlelit evening. Plan the celebration together and then enjoy each other. There will be more than enough days when you'll need to gut through challenges, deal with disappointment, grieve over loss, or just get through one day and onto the next. Mitigate those days by celebrating all the Red Letter Days you can during your life together.

Private Jokes

Private jokes. Code words. Shorthand ways of communicating. They're all part of what makes a couple a couple. To Dale and me, for instance, "not pregnant" means "don't make assumptions." Here's how that one came about: we were on the way to a matinee. I was driving my red-hot Mustang, chatting and not paying attention, when Wham! I rear-ended a van. We pulled into the closest parking lot and while I went to speak to the driver, Dale ran to the other side. He yanked the door open, then blurted out to the large woman reclining in the seat, "Oh, my God, you're really pregnant!"

Problem was, she wasn't. Oops! That day Dale learned a lot about not making assumptions, and we gained a very funny yet pointed phrase of couple-speak.

Once my sister Jenny gave driving instructions to her husband Bill, who was picking her up at a friend's house. She told him to turn *right* on Main, then right on Second. She added helpfully, "After you turn on Main, if you pass Madison you've gone too far." It wasn't until after Bill had driven many miles and still hadn't seen Madison that he called Jenny, only to learn that she should have told him to turn *left* on Main. Now, when one or the other of them is pushing his or her luck in some way, they cue the other with, "You've just passed Madison."

There's a reason why we use the phrase "private joke" to describe these shorthand ways of communicating—they often come from humorous situations. True, the humor is often found only in retrospect. It wasn't until viewed from hindsight that Lila and Matt, the couple you will meet in Chapter 8, laughed at the spilled groceries and adopted the phrase "the potato salad went splat" to mean "I've had a rough day."

It wasn't until Dale made me laugh with his Graham-thinks-I'm-funny comment that I saw the humor in being stuck in the rain forest. Now, years later, when I fail to find Dale as humorous as he thinks he is, I say, "Rain forest." At that point he knows to get serious but before he does, he often adds, "Graham think I'm funny." It always makes me smile.

Here's another example: One Saturday afternoon spouses Rita and Mitchell were each out running errands. She had gone one way, he had gone another—or so they thought until their cars collided in the mall parking lot. Rita immediately saw the humor. She knew, however, that Mitchell, a police officer, would be embarrassed filling out an accident report for a fender bender with his own wife! So, showing great restraint, she kept her laughter to herself, knowing he would eventually come around. He did. A few weeks later, they were with friends who related a story about running into a couple they hadn't seen in years. Mitchell gave Rita a knowing smile and said, "We give new meaning to the phrase 'running into each other,' don't we, honey?" When Mitchell leaves for work, Rita often says, "Don't run into any old friends," which is her way of saying, "Be safe."

Sometimes, seeing the humor is a matter of choice. Once Dale and I decided to get some exercise and walk the 3-mile round trip to the grocery store. We could see rain clouds in the distance. When I speculated on whether we had time to get there and back before the rain came, Dale gave me his I've-been-sailing-for-years-and-know-weather assurance that the rain was many hours away, and I believed him. My mistake. We made it to the supermarket just before the downpour began. We were now faced with a mile-and-a-half walk home in the cats-and-dogs deluge. I was not a happy girl when we stopped at the dry cleaners to beg plastic bags to use as rain gear. Swathed in dry-cleaning bags, we headed out and, of course, were drenched in minutes. I was bent all out of shape and about to say something snippy about Dale's alleged weather-predicting capability when I noticed he had his face turned up and his arms spread wide so he could experience every rain drop. I had taken a "this sucks" point of view. He had taken a "this is great" point of view. Decision time: Stay mad or follow Dale's lead. Easy decision. Before long, we both were dancing in the rain. Now, when rain threatens, one or the other of us will often say, "Better stop at the dry cleaners." To anyone listening, that makes no sense whatever. To us, it triggers the memory of the day we danced in the rain, and that memory always makes us want to hold hands.

To strengthen your bond as a couple, lighten up. Have fun. See the humor. It goes a long way towards helping you create your own private jokes. And, private jokes, code words, things only you understand underscore your "coupleness" like nothing else can. Every time you engage in your own couple-speak, it's like a private and mini-celebration of your togetherness.

Daily Intimacy Rituals

A fabulous relationship has many of the same attributes as a great friendship. When it's working, you can feel the "ka-chunk" as it settles neatly into its place in the universe. There's someone to zip your dress, give an opinion about what tie goes with that jacket, get aspirin for your headache, or laugh at your jokes. Good stuff. But what sustains a committed relationship and makes it GREAT is emotional intimacy. That's what makes living together on a day-to-day basis, with all its ups and downs, easy and comfortable—and why it's important for every couple to have intimacy rituals that can be practiced daily.

No, I don't mean candles, heated massage oil, and the

hot tub. Those are great for sexual intimacy. But let's not confuse physical intimacy with emotional intimacy. In the falling-in-love fireworks stage of your relationship, intimacy equaled SEX! But, over time, things cool down a bit, you settle into your nest, the stork pays a visit or two, there's a lawn to be mowed, the cat has to go to the vet, the kids need chauffeuring or help with homework, the car breaks down, the toilet backs up, one of you loses a job, gets sick, or has an argument with a friend. All of that makes you too tired to think, let alone jump each other's bones.

When the now-less-frequent opportunity for sex presents itself, there will be times when you really do have a headache, are too irritated by your mouthy teenager's attitude, have an early flight to catch, or for whatever reason you're just not in the mood. You cannot rely solely on sex to provide the intimacy you need to have a great relationship. Yes, a good sex life is important, but without emotional intimacy, your relationship is likely to wither and die no matter how great the sex may be.

One of the most important and effective things a couple can do to stay intimate is to talk to each other. I don't mean brief bits of conversation as you fly out the door, texting, or emailing. I mean face-to-face, sit-down-and-talk-to-me time. I realized how important this was in my own marriage when home renovations interrupted our routine. Dale, as you may recall, is the cook in our house. In California, our kitchen was set up so that while Dale cooked I could sit at the breakfast bar, have a cup of coffee or a glass of wine, and we could chat. While our

Virginia home was being remodeled, we had no place for that. In fact, for nearly seven months, we had no kitchen at all unless an electric skillet and coffee pot count as a kitchen. Meals were eaten in front of the TV in the room that served as our den, my office, and our guest room. Then, one night, when the renovations were done, I sat for the first time in our new breakfast nook, had a glass of wine, and we chatted while Dale cooked. We realized how much we had missed that together time and how important it is to our emotional intimacy.

Now, our days start with Dale sitting in the bathroom and chatting with me while I get dressed for the office. We don't talk about anything special. We're just together for a few minutes before we go our separate ways. We come back together in the evening. We don't answer the phone and the TV is off. We talk about current events or Dale's trip to the grocery store where he ran into a friend, we chuckle over something cute a grandchild said, we plan a dinner party, or revisit a favorite memory. An eavesdropper would find it mundane, but for us, it's a reconnection after being apart all day. And, here's the good part: we continuously learn new things about each other as the free-flow conversation goes wherever it goes.

It's easy for Dale and me to find time together because it's just the two of us. Believe me, on those nights when the grandkids sleep over, our evening dinner and the next morning are very different from what I just described. I fully understand that when you have children at home, making time for each other is no small task but it's worth it. Here's what other couples have done:

- Angie and Todd wake 15 minutes earlier than they have to so they have time to snuggle and talk every morning before their busy day begins.

- Jolene and Casey touch base by phone on their lunch hour and often have lunch together.

- Pamela and Will play dominoes every night after the kids go to bed and as they play, they chat.

Intimacy rituals don't have to be complicated or take a big chunk of time. They can even be part of a daily chore or event. For you, an intimacy ritual might be cooking dinner together, praying together, doing an evening crossword puzzle together, taking an evening walk, dressing together in the morning, or turning off the TV and snuggling and chatting for 20 minutes before going to sleep. Phyllis and Brent end their days by sharing with each other their favorite moments of the day so each day ends on a happy note. Nice.

Intimacy rituals are a celebration of your relationship and your togetherness. Take a minute to think about those times when it was just the two of you, and you looked at your sweetheart and thought, "My God, I love this person so much it hurts my heart!" What were you doing? It might have been bathing the baby together, or pulling weeds in the garden while you chatted about seemingly nothing, or spending a few more minutes in bed, snuggling while waking up. Now ask yourself if whatever you were doing can be incorporated into your life as an intimacy ritual.

When you take a few minutes every day to consciously

connect, you'll find yourselves feeling more emotionally intimate all day long.

Memories: The Glue that Binds

The prize for a life lived together is a great big stack of memories—some tragic, some joyful, most falling somewhere in between. Some are memorialized in photo albums that can be pulled off the shelf and revisited. Others are stored in the mind. Some are celebrated with quiet remembrance of how you survived and became stronger as a couple. Others are celebrated with a popped cork. Most are celebrated with a swelling heart and a fond smile.

I wasn't thinking about memories when I Googled the term "romantic gestures." I was writing an article about romance. What popped up was "breakfast in bed" as a classic "oldie but goodie." My first reaction was to think this is weird. After all, you don't sleep on your kitchen table so why would you eat in bed? Then I recalled that one of my favorite memories—the kind that makes you feel all warm and oh-boy-do-I-LOVE-that-guy gushy—involves breakfast in bed.

It was 1998. Dale and I had been traveling in Peru. After 30 days of local cuisine—including Guinea Pig—served on our four-day hike in the Andes, on our five nights of camping in the rain forest, and on floating islands in Lake Titicaca, we would have sold our souls for a hot dog. Our last day was spent in the capital city of Lima. After checking into the hotel, we wandered aimlessly down one street or another. Maybe it was divine intervention, maybe it was just dumb luck, but as we turned a corner, there in the distance glowed the neon sign of a TGIF. Like brood mares who've caught sight of the barn, we headed straight for Buffalo wings, cheese burgers, and Budweiser. It was divine. We thought it couldn't get any better. We were wrong.

Just up the street was a Dunkin' Donuts. The proprietor had locked the door and was cleaning up when he saw us peering through the window, looking like hungry orphans despite having gorged ourselves at TGIF. Taking pity, that wonderful man unlocked the door and sold us a dozen assorted.

The next morning we propped ourselves up in bed, flipped open the donut box, and popped the cork on a bottle of champagne we'd been saving to celebrate our time in Peru. We sipped champagne from plastic hotel glasses and ate the entire dozen donuts before snuggling back under the covers for—well, you know.

Moments like our Peruvian breakfast become treasured memories. They form the glue that binds a couple. While some memories are more momentous than others, shared experiences need not be monumental to be precious. For instance....

Chandler and Chelsea remember the day when, as newlyweds, they planted the rose bushes, now fully matured, as one of their most treasured memories. As they worked together, they shared their dreams about their future, the family they hoped to have, and their aspirations. Now, many years later, they continue to visit the rose garden whenever they need to have The Talk or just want to feel especially close.

Lynette and Gary like to revisit the day when they were on a hike, sat under a tree to enjoy the view, and while holding hands, decided to start a family.

Donna and Karl lost their 10-year-old child to cancer. They certainly don't celebrate the anniversary of the day their sweet girl died as one would celebrate a happy event, but they always observe that day with reverence and gratitude for how they survived her death together and found solace in each other. They celebrate their daughter's birthday with gratitude for the 10 years she was with them.

Rosalie and Kent were in the Peace Corps together and remember fondly the day they strolled the bazaar in a small Kenyan village. Nothing momentous happened that day. It was just a beautiful day that, for whatever reason, resonated with both of them.

My friend Susie and her husband journal, not every day, but when something memorable happens for one them, he or she enters it in the journal that they share. Every so often, they pull the journal off the shelf to see what the other has written and talk about it.

It isn't important that both of you remember and treasure the same things. I recall a day when Dale and I played hooky and spent the day on the California coast. Dale doesn't specifically remember that day, but I remember it as the day when I realized that Dale truly loved me. He was standing on the edge of a cliff, looking out to sea, the wind riffling his hair, and as I watched him from a distance, an internal voice said loudly and clearly, "This man, this wonderful man, truly loves me!"

A life lived together is a complex tapestry of the good and the not-so-good, the joyful and the tragic, the challenges and the triumphs. All couples have ups and downs. Getting through the down times is a lot easier when you harken back to and relive feel-good memories simply by saying, "Hey, remember when...."

Reliving memories is a great way to celebrate your relationship. Regardless of whether your relationship is relatively new or many years old, you have a stockpile of memories. Pull the photo album off the shelf, pour a glass of wine or your favorite beverage, and as you turn the pages, toast yourselves for building a life together.

Let There Be Spaces in Your Togetherness

So far we've talked about celebrating your relationship and the life you've built together. I want to remind you to also celebrate each other as the unique and wonderful individuals that you are. Celebrate what you learn from each other, the ways you complement each other, the ways in which your unique qualities make you stronger as a couple.

Kahlil Gibran in *The Prophet* wrote, "Let there be spaces in your togetherness." Gibran is not suggesting that couples take an occasional breather from each other (although that might be a good idea, too). In beautiful, lyrical language Gibran reminds us not to lose ourselves in our relationship, but to celebrate and maintain our individuality. He also writes, "And stand together, yet not too near together: For the pillars of the temple stand apart...." I would happily trade a valuable body part for the ability to write like Gibran but no one has offered that deal, so I'm stuck with elaborating in my far less lyrical way. "Togetherness" is not about being joined at the hip. "Togetherness" is about the emotional and mental bond that connects you and, like the pillars of the temple, supports you and your relationship even when you are physically separated. It's the reservoir of strength you draw on when you need to be strong. It's the hand at your back when you need encouragement. It's the well of confidence you tap into when your self-belief wavers.

The Gibran passage concludes with, "And the oak tree and the cypress grow not in each other's shadow." "Togetherness" is not about being each other's clone. It's the freedom to be who you are without fear of losing love. It's permission to make mistakes, change and grow. It's willingness to learn at each other's knee. It's recognizing and respecting that each of us has a Foreplay Navigator that is a complex mix of preferences, opinions, priorities, standards, points of view, and sensitivities, all shaped by our DNA, upbringing, education, life's experience, religious or philosophical training, culture and self-perception.

The emotional intimacy that is the hallmark of "togetherness" is akin to being in a state of grace. So the next time you're about to make some snarky comment to your sweetie, or let loose with a piece of your mind, or turn a cold shoulder, or go to that he's-such-a-jerk or she's-such-a-witch place, or "forget" to keep a promise, or shrug off your partner's wishes, or, well, you get the picture, ask yourself if what you're about to say or do will put a chink in your "togetherness." Too many chinks and you'll slip right into "aloneness" and that sucks. Remember, most failed relationships suffer death by a thousand cuts. The little stuff counts big time. Protect and honor your "togetherness" by being thoughtful, kind, loving, generous, supportive, understanding and, well, you get the picture here, too. Consult your Foreplay Back-Pocket Guide and learn as much as you can about your own and your partner's Foreplay Navigator.

Kool and the Gang's song *Celebration* is played at virtually every wedding reception ever held. It's a feel-good song that reminds us that love is to be celebrated. Okay, it's true. Not every day and every moment, of your life together will be a party or the stuff that inspires celebration, but, taken as a whole, it sure as heck is. So, come on, celebrate!

*8

Your Ticket to Total Intimacy

> *Love at first sight is easy to understand;*
> *it's when two people have been looking at each*
> *other for a lifetime that it becomes a miracle.*
>
> —Amy Bloom

I'm often asked the one piece of advice I give all couples. It is this: *Treat every moment as one that will either make or break your relationship.*

In my work with couples, I've learned that most partners step up for the big stuff. But it's not every day you lose a parent, get a PhD, have a fight with your best friend, give birth, or land your dream job. Everyday life is a string of small, often ordinary, events. It's how you handle these that *really* makes or breaks your relationship and determines how intimate it will be. Let me give you an example.

Matt was responsible for preparing a complicated bid on a job for his engineering firm. An ill secretary and a finicky Internet connection were the tip of the what-went-wrong iceberg. With only minutes to spare, Matt hit "send" on the email that submitted the bid. He left exhausted and cranky. Lila, who had a full day of meetings, had that morning asked Matt to pick up dinner. He did. As he walked from the garage to the back door, the food bag broke. The potato salad container burst on contact. The roasted chicken popped out of its box and rolled under a hedge. Lila heard Matt's expletive, rushed to the door, and asked, "What happened?"

Matt snapped.

"What happened?" he yelled. "I dropped dinner. That's what happened! The perfect end to a totally miserable day."

"Why are you yelling at me? It's not my fault," Lila knee-jerk responded.

"If you hadn't insisted I get dinner, this wouldn't have happened," he knee-jerk (albeit irrationally) responded back.

"Oh, so it *is* my fault you had a bad day," she shouted and stormed into the house, leaving Matt to clean up the mess.

These are the moments that short circuit intimacy. Damage from one such moment won't send you to divorce court but it puts you on the road. That's why it's important to avoid them. But none of us is perfect. Despite best efforts, we do imperfect things. It's darned lucky, therefore, that a break can sometimes be turned into a make. After Lila consulted her Foreplay Back-Pocket Guide, she poured two glasses of wine, went back outside, and handed a glass to Matt. She said, "Hey, buddy, you wanna tell me about it?" Matt accepted the peace offering and smiled. Lila understood that Matt had spoken out of frustration. He understood she had responded accordingly. Both knew that neither had meant to hurt the other. No apologies were necessary. Intimacy was re-established.

Short temper, bad moods, impatience, knee-jerk responses, these all come with being human in a crazy busy world. Moments such as that experienced by Matt and Lila are inevitable. The choice is yours whether such moments are left as break or are turned into make. Smart couples choose the latter.

Relax. You don't have to be perfect.

You don't have to meet an impossible standard to be a Totally Intimate couple. Since none of us is perfect, it's a darned good thing that what's required is within reach of all of us, and that is:

- Acceptance that *inadvertent* breaks in intimacy occur.

- A mutual commitment to convert a break to a make.

- Mutual trust that neither partner will *deliberately* cause a break.

As you learned in Chapter 1, most relationships that fail suffer death by a thousand cuts. Any relationship older than a week has suffered a cut here and a cut there. It's inevitable. But nothing cuts more deeply and destroys intimacy more quickly than deliberately hurtful acts—infidelity, physical abuse, name-calling, belittling comments, indifference to your partner's needs, lack of courtesy, disrespect, and blatant disregard for your sweetheart's feelings and wishes. Such behavior may be forgiven, *but it is not forgotten.* The damage can never be completely eliminated. Picture the woman with a split lip courtesy of her husband's fist. He may be truly sorry, and she may truly forgive him, but she'll never forget. When your body is wounded, it is unable to produce the same healthy tissue that is damaged. To protect itself, the body forms scar tissue, but that is weaker and inferior to the healthy tissue it replaces. The same is true of emotional wounds. They may heal, but what remains is emotional scar tissue.

A steady diet of forgiveness leads to an unhealthy relationship.

A relationship is dynamic. It is shaped, molded and defined by everything that happens to it. When it is nurtured and cherished, it is strong and enduring, capable of withstanding challenges. But a relationship that survives on repeated forgiveness is fragile and unhealthy, riddled by scar tissue. Forgiveness is essential to all relationships. But it is not unconditional. It comes with the tacit understanding that if the hurtful behavior happens too many more times, forgiveness is revoked and the relationship will end.

Although it is possible for a relationship to survive, even thrive, after a major body blow such as infidelity, my advice is this: If you want a Totally Intimate relationship, treat every moment as one that either cracks your relationship or makes it stronger. Avoid doing those things for which an apology and forgiveness are required.

Total Intimacy is yours for the taking.

Let's review the elements of Total Intimacy:

You are so connected in mind and heart you feel a physical bond. I could give you a chemistry lesson in the neuroscience of love but who (besides a neuroscientist) cares about the oozing hormones that make love a physically manifested emotion. But get this: Research shows that when you have sex, the brain releases a hormone that makes you bond. How cool is that?

And there's more. People in satisfying relationships have better physical and mental health than those who are not. They have greater longevity, fewer injuries from accidents, less stress, lower blood pressure, stronger immune systems, and increased brain activity in regions associated with feelings of calmness and pain suppression.

In short, being in a great relationship is darned good for you. Nature gets you started on the right track. In the early days, when you're having all that can't-get-enough-of-you sex, your brain is quietly doing its job creating the bond that is the essence of intimacy. It's in your enlightened self-interest to protect and strengthen the bond that nature offers. When your Frequent Foreplay Miles account balances are waaaaay up there, your emotional bond will inspire one irresistible urge after another to touch, hold hands, kiss, and, well, you know.

It's totally cool to share your most private thoughts, needs and desires. Nothing is more intimate than when sweethearts bare their emotions, brave exposure, and bestow and receive the priceless gift of trust. It's the kind of trust where you feel safe in the knowledge that your partner will not think less of you because of what you share and will not take advantage of your vulnerability. I have that trust in Dale. Never was his reciprocal trust more evident than during a sensitive discussion we had while fighting our way back from the financial loss and upheaval I talked about in Chapter 1.

When describing how overwhelmed he was by the remodeling project, and how sad and unhappy he was feeling about the circumstances that led to our move, Dale said, "I find that I don't love you with the same spirit of joy that I once did." I initially reacted as any spouse would. My heart raced, I got lightheaded, and I was fearful he wanted out of our marriage. I said nothing. I gave myself time to settle down and think. What Dale said was delivered with such profound sadness, that I soon realized he wasn't telling me he wanted out. He was telling me he wanted *back*. What's more, his honesty forced me to face that my feelings for him had also changed. That was the moment we acknowledged our relationship was in trouble. We together pledged to recapture the spirit of joy we once felt. I don't know what would have happened had we not trusted each other with those feelings, but I do believe the chances of our happily surviving would have been less.

Can you recall a time when your sweetheart trusted you with a secret fear, hope, or hurt? Maybe it was something embarrassing or your sweetheart regretted, or a painful experience from childhood, or a fear of something he or she is facing, or a dream of doing something different. It felt good to be trusted, didn't it? Now give your sweetheart Frequent Foreplay Miles for that gift.

And, remember, such trust is fragile. It is jeopardized, perhaps lost, when you fail to treasure your sweetheart's trust as the priceless gift that it is. Frequent Foreplay Miles and your Foreplay Back-Pocket Guide help you do just that.

You are 24/7 cheerleaders—nurturing, loving, and supportive—so you become the best that you can be. When there's dry cleaning to pick up, groceries to buy, a dog to walk, a UPS truck that's expected,

165

a lawn that needs mowing, a kid with a tummy ache, a plugged up toilet, bills to pay, windows to wash, and dinner to prepare, having someone share the load makes life a lot easier. The same is true when you're down in the dumps, crossing your fingers for a promotion, coaching your kid's soccer team, facing a medical procedure, writing a book (that's a BIG one), feeling disappointed by a friend, unhappy on the job, irritated with yourself for getting a speeding ticket, worried about a failing parent, at your wit's end over your teenager's attitude, or starting an MBA program.

Getting through the rough spots of life is easier when there's someone propping you up, lending strength, and believing in you. Sometimes you have to accomplish something extra, pushing yourself further, and stretching beyond where you thought you could. These challenges are easier when there's somebody on your side who believes in you, gently nudges you forward, cheers you on, and has button-bursting pride in your accomplishments.

Frequent Foreplay Miles helps you be that somebody for each other. When you're nurtured, loved and supported you can't help but be better, stretch further, and do more than you ever thought possible.

You trust that even when mess-ups happen, you've both acted with good intentions. No matter how hard you try, you will mess up. You will both forget to consult your Foreplay Back-Pocket Guide. You will speak before you think. Your Foreplay Navigators will take you in the wrong direction. And each of you will occasionally do something so clueless the other will wonder if you've suffered a head injury. It is unreasonable to demand perfection. It *is* reasonable to expect that your sweetheart will not intentionally hurt you.

A seminar attendee once challenged me on this point. She argued, "If I'm walking down the street and a driver deliberately aims for me, I get hurt when I'm hit. If a driver swerves to avoid hitting a child and hits me, I get hurt. The intention is different but the result is the same. If my partner hurts me deliberately or unintentionally, I'm still hurt."

She was right that the hurt is real. The difference is in the penalty. I explained it by reverting to my legal roots. The guy who *deliberately* hits you is guilty of felony assault and punished accordingly. The guy who *inadvertently* hits you isn't. He's not going to jail and his insurance covers the medical bills.

I'm not suggesting you shouldn't feel hurt or disappointed when your partner inadvertently messes up. But if it's not a felony, don't treat it as one. Consider Frequent Foreplay Miles as your insurance, a reserve of good will to cover the damage from unintentional hurts.

As an added bonus, you want to jump each other's bones at every opportunity! I don't really need to say a lot about this one, do I? An intimate and rewarding sex life just naturally results from "all of the above."

Dale and I had our first date on September 4, 1996, and became inseparable. Dale told me he was in love on Super Bowl Sunday, January 26, 1997. I was crazy mad about him. We were married on February 20, 1999. We've long ago stopped worrying about being caught wearing sweats, with unshaven beard (in his case) or unshaven legs (in my case), with bed hair, or unbrushed teeth. Gravity and time have taken their toll on both of us. The intense sexual excitement of our early days has been replaced with easy comfort, quiet affection and profound love. Still, when I look at him across a crowded room, he takes my breath away and I can't believe what a lucky woman I am.

Our path to Total Intimacy was not without obstacles. We faced down the challenge that rocked our marriage to the core. We know up-close-and-personal that the next challenge may be around the corner. We survived once by staying true to our Frequent Foreplay Miles philosophy of marriage. We can do it again. You can, too.

Assume the best about your sweetheart. Act with the best of intentions. Put a muzzle on knee-jerk negative feelings and spin in a positive direction. Examine your own Foreplay Navigator—change the things that need changing, fix what needs to be fixed. Learn as much about your sweetheart's Foreplay Navigator as you can. Where it differs from yours, keep an open mind. Let go of "right and wrong." Understand that head butting, toe stepping and wire crossing are inevitable. Look for ways to earn Frequent Foreplay Miles. Look for ways to give them to your sweetie. Refer often to your Foreplay Back-Pocket Guide. Remember that words hurt, they hurt a lot and once uttered can never be taken back. Be careful how you use them. Earn and give trust.

We've come to the end of our time together. My wish for you is that with Frequent Foreplay Miles you'll have the Totally Intimate relationship I know you want, and that you'll also have fun along the way. I hope you'll stay in touch by visiting my blog and website at www.Frequent-ForeplayMiles.com and that you'll also feel free to contact me directly through the "Contact Us" page of the site.

And remember that it is the balance of kindness to hurt that determines the daily and long-term health of your relationship.

Kind and thoughtful acts mitigate the damage done by head butts, stepped on toes, and crossed wires. Better yet, they wrap the heart in a protective shield of love, making it less vulnerable to wounds. As I was working on this book, Dale one day walked into my office with a plump, red-ripe strawberry. As he handed it to me, he said, "So you'll have a bright spot in your day." I'll never again look at a perfectly ripe strawberry without thinking of how, with that simple gesture, my sweetheart made me feel loved and supported. Tell your sweetie, "I love you." It's nice to hear. But as William Shakespeare said, "Action is eloquence." Sometimes, it's the simplest thing—like a ripe strawberry—that is the most eloquent:

- Surprise your sweetheart with the coconut cake she adores, a book he said he'd like to read, the body lotion she loves but won't buy for herself, or tickets to a concert that will transport him back to his college days.

- Compliment your partner on what a great dad he is or what a fabulous cook she is.

- Plant her favorite daffodils in the garden.

- Record a TV show your honey will enjoy but will miss because of working late.

- Understand that sometimes your partner really is too tire.

- Share your chocolate chip cookie.

- Fix tomato soup when your sweetheart has a cold.

- Acknowledge how sexy he looks in his tuxedo or she looks in her party dress.

- Brag to friends about his golf score or the watercolor she did in art class.

The little things count. Big Time. If you keep that in mind and look for daily ways to say, "I love you," your Frequent Foreplay Miles account will be over the moon before you know it.

Total Intimacy. It's yours for the taking.
Now, go get it!

Appendices

*frequent*
foreplay*miles*

Back-Pocket Guide

How can I **LOCK** in Frequent Foreplay Miles?

How can I help my sweetheart **ACE** Frequent Foreplay Miles?

How can I **NAVIGATE** from negative spin to positive spin?

What can I **DO** so we both earn Frequent Foreplay Miles?

Make a perfect 3-point **LAND**ing every time!

 *frequent foreplay miles*

Generosity Generator

Instructions

Complete each sentence with an example of something that made you
feel as described. Then explain why you chose this example.
Feel free to give more than one example but the total Frequent Foreplay Miles
awarded for each will be 100 regardless of how many examples you give.
Don't try too hard! Just let your mind go where it goes.

Statement		FFM
One of my favorite memories of a time with my sweetheart is . . .		100
I felt supported by my sweetheart when . . .		100
I felt appreciated by my sweetheart when . . .		100
I wanted to shout for joy when my sweetheart . . .		100
I was grateful when my sweetheart . . .		100
I really felt the love when my sweetheart . . .		100

174

Tracker
Instructions

If this is the first Frequent Foreplay Miles Tracker you've used, enter the 600 Frequent Foreplay Miles you awarded to your sweetheart in your Generosity Generator as the Beginning Balance. If you haven't completed the Generosity Generator, now is a good time to do so. If you'd rather just get started, then enter zero as the Beginning Balance.

If this is not the first Tracker you've completed, enter the ending balance of your sweetheart's Frequent Foreplay Miles account from the previous week's Tracker as the Beginning Balance. When you complete the first page of this week's Tracker, calculate the Page Total, i.e., the Beginning Balance plus each Tracker entry, and carry that balance forward to the next page. Start a new Tracker every week. Carry the previous week's ending balance forward to the new Tracker as the Beginning Balance.

For detailed instructions on Tracking, please refer to Chapter 4. Use the following table as the guide for how many Frequent Foreplay Miles to award or deduct. Select the emotion that most accurately describes how your sweetheart's behavior made you feel. You may give bonus Frequent Foreplay Miles or make a penalty deduction. If you do, explain why.

Emotion	Frequent Foreplay Miles Award	Emotion	Frequent Foreplay Miles Deduction
Ecstatic	100	Annoyed	-25
Overjoyed	90	Irritated	-30
Supported	80	Aggravated	-35
Thrilled	75	Angry	-45
Delighted	60	Hurt	-55
Happy	50	Disappointed	-65
Grateful	45	Furious	-75
Proud	40	Brokenhearted	-85
Pleased	35	Homicidal	-90
Touched	30	Devastated	-100

The more detailed your explanation, the more you will understand and communicate your Foreplay Navigator. Be generous in awarding Frequent Foreplay Miles and slow to deduct them. Remember, rarely does your sweetheart intend to hurt, disappoint or anger you.

Most of all, make it fun!

 *frequent foreplay miles*

Tracker
Page 1

Week of [　　　　　] Beginning Balance [　　　　　]

Behavior & Why Frequent Foreplay Miles were awarded or deducted.	Emotion

FFM　　　+/-

Total

FFM　　　+/-

Total

FFM　　　+/-

Total

Page Total

frequent
foreplay *miles*

Tracker
Page 2

Balance Carried Forward

Behavior & Why Frequent Foreplay Miles were awarded or deducted.	Emotion

	FFM	+/-
	Total	

	FFM	+/-
	Total	

	FFM	+/-
	Total	

Page Total

 *frequent foreplay miles*

 Certificate of Award

Dear Sweetheart,

You have been awarded Frequent Foreplay Miles in the amount of:

I gave you these Frequent Foreplay
Miles because . . .

You may redeem these Frequent
Foreplay Miles for . . .

178

frequent
foreplay *miles*

Tip Sheet

Dear Sweetheart,

Looking for ways to earn Frequent Foreplay Miles? Here are some ideas.

```
┌─────────────────────────────────────────────────────────────┐
│                                                             │
└─────────────────────────────────────────────────────────────┘

┌─────────────────────────────────────────────────────────────┐
│                                                             │
└─────────────────────────────────────────────────────────────┘

┌─────────────────────────────────────────────────────────────┐
│                                                             │
└─────────────────────────────────────────────────────────────┘

┌─────────────────────────────────────────────────────────────┐
│                                                             │
└─────────────────────────────────────────────────────────────┘

┌─────────────────────────────────────────────────────────────┐
│                                                             │
└─────────────────────────────────────────────────────────────┘

┌─────────────────────────────────────────────────────────────┐
│                                                             │
└─────────────────────────────────────────────────────────────┘
```

Breinigsville, PA USA
16 September 2010
245457BV00006B/1/P